IAN McEWAN

THE INNOCENT

**Hear for yourself the seductive brilliance of
Ian McEwan's new novel at his readings in May:**

8 May	**DUBLIN**	— Waterstone's Booksellers, 7.30pm
10 May	**OXFORD**	— Blackwell's Bookshop, 7.30pm
11 May	**LONDON**	— Royal National Theatre Lyttleton Auditorium, 6.00pm
16 May	**MANCHESTER**	— Royal National College of Music, in association with Waterstone's Booksellers, 7.30pm
17 May	**EDINBURGH**	— Waterstone's Booksellers, 7.30pm
18 May	**GLASGOW**	— Boyd Orr Building, Glasgow University, in association with John Smith's Booksellers, 7.30pm
21 May	**BRISTOL**	— Watershed Media Centre, 7.30pm

JONATHAN CAPE

MELVYN BRAGG

A Time to Dance

"Astounding ... This is a book of splendours and treacheries, pungent as any consuming passion, a great, tragic, raunchy book ..."
Thomas Keneally

£12.95

Hodder & Stoughton *Publishers*

HISTORY

32

Editor: Bill Buford
Guest Editor: Bob Tashman
Commissioning Editor: Lucretia Stewart
Assistant Editor: Tim Adams
Managing Editor: Angus MacKinnon
Assistant to the Editor: Ursula Doyle

Managing Director: Caroline Michel
Circulation Director: Sarah Bristow
Financial Controller: Michael Helm
Publishing Assistant: Sally Lewis
Subscriptions: Gillian Kemp, Carol Harris
Office Assistant: Stephen Taylor

Picture Editor: Alice Rose George
Picture Research: Sally Lewis
Design: Chris Hyde
Executive Editor: Pete de Bolla
US Associate Publisher: Anne Kinard, Granta, 250 West 57th Street, Suite 1316, New York, NY 10107.

Editorial and Subscription Correspondence: Granta, 2–3 Hanover Yard, Noel Road, Islington, London N1 8BE. Telephone: (071) 704 9776. Fax: (071) 704 0474. Subscriptions: (071) 704 0470.
A one-year subscription (four issues) is £19.95 in Britain, £25.95 for the rest of Europe, and £31.95 for the rest of the World.
All manuscripts are welcome but must be accompanied by a stamped, self-addressed envelope or they cannot be returned.

Granta is photoset by Cambridge Photosetting Services, Cambridge, England, and printed by BPCC Hazell Books Ltd, Aylesbury, Bucks.

Granta is published by Granta Publications Ltd and distributed by Penguin Books Ltd, Harmondsworth, Middlesex, England; Viking Penguin Inc., 40 West 23rd St, New York, New York, USA; Penguin Books Australia Ltd, Ringwood, Victoria, Australia; Penguin Books Canada Ltd, 2801 John Street, Markham, Ontario, Canada L3R 1B4; Penguin Books (NZ) Ltd, 182–90 Wairau Road, Auckland 10, New Zealand. This selection copyright © 1990 by Granta Publications Ltd.

Cover by the Senate. Photos: Ronald Grant Archive (John Wayne) and Robert Haas (New York).

Granta 32, Summer 1990

ISBN 014-01-3857-9

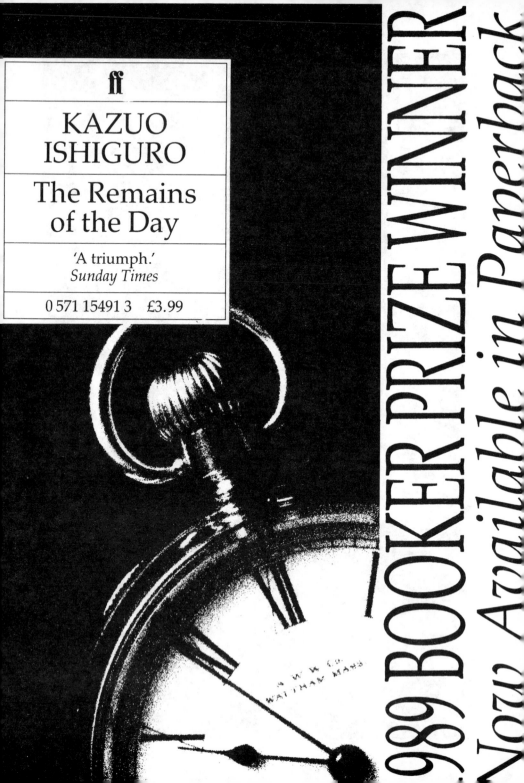

ff

KAZUO ISHIGURO

The Remains of the Day

'A triumph.'
Sunday Times

0 571 15491 3   £3.99

1989 BOOKER PRIZE WINNER

Now Available in Paperback

CONTENTS

Cambridge

Nations and Nationalism since 1780

Programme, Myth, Reality

E.J. HOBSBAWM

Nationalism has become *the* issue of the '90s. In this timely new book Britain's most respected historian examines the concept of nationalism and its relevance to modern states. He dispells the myths that surround national identity and places modern nations in their historical perspective. A surprising new book which will provoke passionate debate.

£14.95 net   HB   0 521 33507 8   200 pp.

Ireland 1912–1985

Politics and Society

J.J LEE

' . . . one of the great books of our time . . . (this) brilliant Jeremiad . . . proves once again that Ireland is a fascinating country since it has given birth to such a fascinating book.'   Owen Dudley Edwards,
New Statesman and Society

'There are times in the life of this book reviewer when he is so excited and inspired by a book that he would like it to become compulsory reading for everyone. This is such a time. This is such a book.   *The Cork Examiner*

£14.95 net   PB   0 521 37741 2   852 pp.
£55.00 net   HB   0 521 26648 3

Marc Bloch

A Life in History

CAROLE FINK

'Virtually every European historian has a warm place in his or her heart for Marc Bloch, the eminent French scholar, soldier and Resistance leader who was murdered by pro-Nazi collaborators in 1944. Carole Fink's well-researched, sympathetic biography, the first in any language, reminds us why.'   *The New York Times*

£25.00 net   0 521 37300 X   380 pp.

Cambridge University Press

The Edinburgh Building, Cambridge CB2 2RU, UK.

CITIZENS

A CHRONICLE OF THE
FRENCH REVOLUTION

SIMON SCHAMA

'The most marvellous book I have read about the
French Revolution in the last fifty years'
– Richard Cobb in *The Times*

All that is solid
Melts into air

As dictators fall, borders disappear, walls crumble and social systems come tumbling down map out the world of post-communism with Marxism Today.

Marxism Today **is an open, unpredictable read that mixes politics, culture and style.** Marxism Today **charted the rise of Thatcherism, set the pace in the radical rethink needed for a revival of the Left, and is uniquely placed to track the aftermath of the democratic revolutions of Eastern Europe.**

From post-communism to postmodernism a Marxism Today **subscription is your monthly invite to Unconventional Wisdom.**

New fiction from Constable

Francis King

Pennie Hedge

Paul Sayer

Simon Mason

FRANCIS KING
Visiting cards

'One of the finest contemporary novelists . . . prolific, fluent, witty and moving . . . a master novelist' Melvyn Bragg, *Punch* (£11.95)

PENNIE HEDGE
Moving on

'(Her) buccaneering novel has uninhibited originality and vivid diction' Neil McKenna, *Observer* (£11.95)

PAUL SAYER
Howling at the moon

'Sayer has a remarkable skill in depicting the highly individual yet totally recognisable landscapes of hell' Judy Cooke, *Guardian* (£10.95)

SIMON MASON
The great English nude

'The blackest sexicomedy of the year' David Hughes, *Mail on Sunday* (£11.95)

Constable
1890 · 1990

SIMON SCHAMA
THE MANY DEATHS
OF GENERAL WOLFE

George Townshend, *Portrait of James Wolfe* (1759).

1. At the Face of the Cliff

Anse du Foulon, Quebec, four a.m. 13 September 1759.

'Twas the darkness that did the trick, black as tar, that and the silence, though how the men contriv'd to clamber their way up the cliff with their musket and seventy rounds on their backs, I'm sure I don't know even though I saw it with my own eyes and did it myself before very long. We stood hushed on the muddy shore of the river, peering up at the volunteers. They looked like a pack of lizards unloosd on the rocks, though not so nimble, bellies hugging the cliff and their rumps wiggling with the effort. We couldn't see much of 'em for they disappeared now and then into the clumps of witherd cedar and spruce that hung on the side of the hill. But we could feel the squirming, pulling labour of it all. And by God they were quiet alright. Now and then a man's boot would find a foothold he thought secure and away would come a shower of soft dirt, near taking the fellow with him down the cliff. Curses come to a soldier as easy as breathing, but we heard none that night, not at the start of it all. Some scoundrel later put it about that the General himself had struck off the head of a man who curs'd too loud when he dropped his pack to still any who should think to do the same. But that was never the General's way. Though he had the temper in him of a red-hair'd man he was an orderly commander who lik'd things done by the Regulations and it would go damnd hard on any poor infantryman who thought to help himself to the spoils of war, be it just a goat or a pig, when all the killing and running were done.

I suppose the silence told Wolfe the game was in earnest. For had bodies come tumbling down or firing started from the top he would have stopped it right there and then. For all his soldierly zeal he was rattled by the cliff when he had jumpd from the landing boat and come to its face, and could see the height of it, near enough two hundred feet and the sheerness of it. 'I dont think we can by any possible means get up here,' we heard him say, 'but we must use our best endeavour.' And so it fell to the turn of the Twenty-Eighth and we started to haul ourselves over the black limestone, reaching for stumps and scrubby patches of choke-cherries and hawthorn that covered the nether part of the hill. By such cumbersome means we lugged ourselves up a bit at a time, skinning our hands, dirtying our breeches and praying the next bit of scrawny stick and leaf was deep enough rooted to hold us up. One thing was sure, our coats and leggings weren't made for such work, for they flapped and pinchd as we dragged ourselves up; and I could swear the Rangers who were fitter dress'd for it sniggerd as they saw us struggling with our tackle. Indeed the whole business seemd perilous, vertical folly and nothing the King of Prussia would have commended. We all feard it might yet go badly as it had done in July at the Montmorency Falls where French had peppered us with grapeshot and the drenching rain had turned the hill into a filthy slide. Men had come tumbling down in a mess of blood and mud and fear and those that couldn't run were left to face the Savages as best they could, poor beggars.

But our fortunes were fairer that night for when the sentries challengd our boats as we saild up river Mr Fraser he answered them in French good enough to pass and even threw in an oath or two against the English *bougres* for good measure. And we were all glad of the Scotchmen this time, even the Highlanders, for of Delaune's first men up the rocks they were all Macphersons and Macdougals and Camerons and the like. A good crew for a general who had fought on Culloden Field! And here too they did the King good service for I had no sooner got to the very top and was rejoicing and taking good care not to look down behind me when our men gathered together amidst the tamaracks and the spruce. Before us were a group of tents, white in the first thin light of the coming dawn and of a sudden a commotion and shouting broke forth. A Frenchy officer came flying out in his nightshirt as we loosd off our first rounds and sent them running across the open fields towards the town leaving a few of their company shot or stuck with our bayonets wearing that surprisd look on their face as they lay there amidst the pine needles and brown grass.

Once the peace was broken and we were masters of the place and the French guns we set up a huzzaing and men down below threw themselves at the hill, Wolfe first of all, they said, and suddenly the rocks were alive with soldiers, Rangers and Highlanders and Grenadiers groping their way to the top. Monckton even managed to find a zig-zag path, two men wide, to lug our field pieces up. The boats that had dischargd the first men went back to fetch some more from the ships and after an hour or two we stood in the dawn light, a cool spraying rain coming down, maybe 4,000 of us, more than we had dar'd hope but not so many I still thought as would come to a prize fight at Bartholomews Fair, too few for the business.

Monckton and Barré formd us up again in our lines, smartly enough. The Grenadiers formed to our right and the Forty-Third, Forty-Seventh and the Highlanders to our left, Mr Burton's Forty-Eighth behind us in reserve and Townshend and the Fifteenth at right angles. Better though our situation was than we might have expected, there was not a man jack of us but didnt feel the scare of the battle crawling through his uniform and was glad of the two days rum we had got issued. The General put some heart in us, coming to our lines to talk of duty and the King and what our country expected of us and all of Canada at our mercy if we but prevaild this once. After he died they made him look like a Roman, even on the penny prints I have seen, but he lookd no Roman to us. For though he was six foot, he carried that height queerly, in a loping gait, with his bony frame and sloping shoulders ending in a poke-up neck. What was on top of it bore little resemblance to the Antiques either, what with his popeyes and his little chins wobbling under his jaw, his skin the colour of cheese and a snout on him like a ferret. Nor was he much a humorous man, more in the melancholy way. Brigadier Townshend did some scribbles of him peering at the latrines or measuring the height of his reputation which got passed around the camp and gave us some mirth in the midst of all our adversities, but they pleasd their subject not at all. Yet he was a good general to trust, even if it was his fancy to call us 'brother soldiers', for he was fearless and would walk before the men under fire, pointing his cane like Old Gideon's staff and we followed sure enough.

The Life of General Wolfe

By seven o'clock the low clouds and drizzle that hung over the Heights of Abraham had given way to a gentle sunshine. Wolfe and his three brigadiers—Murray, the dependable Monckton and the erratic Townshend—had placed their lines in battle order. For the first time in the whole campaign, it was the British who waited, the French who had to react. A stillness descended on the grassy plain, broken only by the occasional crack of musket fire coming from Indian and Canadian shooters hidden in the woods to the left of the British lines.

For James Wolfe it had come to this, at last. Months of misery and frustration, of failing to winkle out Montcalm's troops from their citadel of Quebec, much less dislodging the batteries on the north shore of the St. Lawrence, had finally found some resolution. The humiliation of his position had galled him and he was not eased by the embarrassing recollection of drunken, swaggering, boasts made to William Pitt on the eve of his departure. Once up the river he had realized how daunting his mission was; how idle the hope of dividing Montcalm's army or provoking it to come down from its fortified heights and engage. Nor had his proclamation, written, he thought, in the most sententious French at his command, been effective even though it had exuded magnanimity and had spoken honourably of the protection of the Canadians' religion and their property, and given an assurance that he had come not 'to destroy and depopulate' but merely to 'subdue' and 'bring them into subjection to the King his master.' In vexation he had begun to bombard Quebec from the positions set up by the fleet, so that a steady deafening rain of mortars and shells fell on the town, day and night.

But what good had this done except to assuage the endless sense of impotence and rage that swelled inside him as spring turned into a scorching, dripping, foul-smelling summer? His troops were falling sick from putrid fevers and were tormented by blackfly that from their stinging bites could cover a man's face or arms with gobs of blood. When it became apparent that so far from joining themselves to the protection of His Majesty the Canadian trappers and farmers had sent their women and children to the town, while the men had formed irregular companies to harass the troops, a second proclamation, angrier than the first, announced the coming of 'violent' measures both to punish and deter. Farm cabins and whole villages had been destroyed, corn burned in the fields. But in return they had the Indians—Abenakis and Iroquois—to contend with, laying in wait for their raiding parties. And of what the

Savages were said and known to do, their scalping and tomahawking, the troops were in shuddering terror. Men returned to camp unmanned, with stories of slivers of wood pushed up their penis and behind their nails and more than ever they came to feel they were being sacrificed to some vanity of the General and his thirst for reputation.

So the landing at the Montmorency Falls had been determined as much by the need to do *something* to force the issue, as by any calculated hope of success. Wolfe was agonized by the possibility of returning to England not in a chorus of Handelian Hosannas but a cloud of ignominy. How would he dare face Amherst, the commander of the expedition, or Pitt, who had been so criticized for putting his faith in a stripling major-general, still in his thirties? He dreaded the jeering of the merciless coffee-house press; the caricaturists for whom his peculiar physiognomy must have seemed heaven-sent; the howling catcalls of the theatre as some half-drunk actor bawled a profane air at his expense. How could he greet his betrothed who overlooked his curious phiz and figure and his graceless manner as the eccentricities of one born for an heroic fate? How could he look his father, the General, in the eye, and worst of all what would he say to his exacting, adamant mother?

But the landing had been horribly botched. The French had prudently refused to descend to engage their force and had been content to inflict a murderous fire from their batteries on the haplessly climbing soldiers, defenceless and falling over each other in rain-sodden confusion. Painfully aware that he was losing the authority of his command, each day watching his force being eaten up by sickness, boredom and desertion, Wolfe increasingly kept his own counsel and brooded sourly on the disappointment of his hopes. The chivalrous major-general who had exchanged cases of wine with his adversary, the Marquis de Montcalm, who had promised peace and conciliation, now displayed fits of vindictive petulance. Orders were given sending raids deeper into the country to exterminate Canadian settlements at the same time as British guns were obliterating the timbered houses of Old Quebec itself.

Wolfe was running two races and in both, time seemed to be against him. Unless he found some way to pry the French army from its lair, the swift icing of the St. Lawrence would close his fleet in and cut its supply line from the Louisbourg peninsula at the river's mouth. But there was a greater enemy than the river and the season; greater yet than the damnably canny Montcalm, and that was his own body. He had always been preoccupied by his physical frailty and had even been capable of dark banter on the subject. 'If I Say I am thinner,' he had written to his friend Rickson, 'you will imagine me a shadow or a skeleton in motion. In short I am everything but what the surgeons call a subject for anatomy. As far as muscles, bones and the larger vessels conserve their purpose they have a clear view of them in me, distinct from fat or fleshy impediment . . . '

But now, he thought, he was dying, withering away of gravel and consumption; a raging, scalding venom that ate at his guts. His bladder was a failing vessel, his kidneys, demons that racked him day and night. It was torture to piss and worse not to piss and periodically he suffered the indignities of dysentery too. Somehow, though, he grimly preserved his composure, for the sake of his men and for the duty he had taken on. The surgeon bled him profusely and together with his want of sleep, there arose in his naturally wan features a ghostly mouldy pallor from which big eyes glittered in their darkened sockets.

An escape from this death by degrees—of both the expedition itself and its commander—finally presented itself (as escapes so often do) by way of a response to a secondary problem. Thinking of how to intercept Quebec's supply lines from Montreal, to the west, Wolfe's officers and Admiral Saunders, the commander of the fleet, conceived the plan of a sailing up-river, past Quebec itself, to a point where a force might interpose itself between the city and its rear. Wolfe himself needed persuading, all the more so since he increasingly mistrusted one of his three Brigadiers, the overtly disaffected George Townshend whose natural irreverence and sardonic manner was, Wolfe thought, coming damnably close to insubordination. Once convinced of the idea of an attack from behind, Wolfe converted it from a tactical element in the campaign to the strategy on which victory or defeat would necessarily turn. The risks were alarming since the known landing-sites were heavily fortified with batteries, and wherever the guns were less in evidence, the escarpment seemed too sheer to allow any kind of ascent. The only chance of success lay with careful subterfuge and surprise. A flotilla of boats was to go up-river with the flood tide, beyond its apparent landing, and then allow the ebb, calculated for four in the morning, to drift landing-craft back to the shore. But such was Wolfe's mounting mistrust and anxiety, that he refused to divulge to his own senior officers the exact location of this landing, forcing them to write to him for an answer so the plan would not be put in jeopardy.

Wolfe was painfully conscious that the moment that beckoned him was one to which his whole life had been pointing. Since he was a child he had known nothing, nor expected anything, other than the army career in which his father had achieved some rank and modest renown. James had left for camp when he was fourteen, had been an adjutant at Dettingen at sixteen where two horses had been shot from under him and at nineteen had eagerly joined the slaughter of Jacobites at Culloden and Falkirk. Yet nothing much had come of these youthful exertions. He had ended up quartered in Ireland, grumbling in a prematurely bilious way about the corruption, debauchery and insolence of the natives. The coming of another war with France in 1756 seemed to offer liberation from boredom and hypochondria, but instead it enfolded him in fiasco. The amphibious expedition to the Atlantic port of Rochefort had ended up bobbing indeterminately in the roadstead while the naval commander bickered with the army commander on what to do and when to do it. Wolfe was one of the few officers exonerated in the subsequent investigation and was promoted to Brigadier for the siege of Louisbourg at the mouth of the St. Lawrence, French Canada's lifeline to its homeland. While that stronghold eventually fell in 1758, Wolfe regarded the siege as wasteful, prolonged and incompetent and lost no opportunity in letting this be known when he returned on leave at the end of that year.

His reputation had remained unsullied, indeed had even blossomed as the British imperial war effort staggered from mishap to mishap. When William Pitt, the gouty, bloody-minded genius of global strategy, designed one for America of crushing simplicity, Wolfe was given a commission of crucial significance. There would be a two-pronged onslaught on French America that would be decisive: one to the fort of Ticonderoga in the Appalachians, and an amphibious expedition up the St. Lawrence to Quebec and Montreal. If successful, the two attacks would join at the upper Ohio and sever the line of containment France had constructed from Canada to the Mississippi basin against the westward expansion of the British colonies.

Wolfe had always hungered for such a responsibility, but now that it had come, it seemed more a burden than an opportunity. Perhaps Pitt had recognized in him a fellow neurotic, driven by the volatile mixture of monomania, dejection and elation that fired all the most formidable military imperialists. Exactly to type, Wolfe alternated between undignified self-congratulation and self-reproach. He was, he thought, riddled with shortcomings that would be his undoing. His physique deteriorated sympathetically with this onset of mercurial energy and sent him to Bath to take the waters. It was there that he met Katherine Lowther, handsome, articulate and rich, the daughter of the Governor of Barbados (where one became very rich indeed), who was abominated almost everywhere else.

Wolfe had been in love once before, at twenty-one when he had paid court to Elizabeth Lawson (as plain as Katherine Lowther was good-looking); though 'sweet-tempered', she was seriously disabled in the eyes of General and Mrs Wolfe by her modest fortune. They had made their own selection for their son, which he in turn rejected. Parents and son then compromised by forgetting about marriage altogether. Once hot with passion, Wolfe cooled rapidly as he distanced himself from his love and got on with war and advancement. He was ten years older when he met Katherine; she commanded a rank and fortune that Wolfe must have presumed would sweep aside any parental reservations. He was sadly disabused of this unwarranted optimism. Henrietta Wolfe remained implacable in her displeasure, unmoveable in her objections. A frosty hostility descended on a relationship which until recently had been suffocatingly close. Wolfe visited the family house at Blackheath just once during his three-month winter leave and instead of bidding his parents farewell sent a letter of bleak severity to his mother:

DEAR MADAM,—The formality of taking leave should be as much as possible avoided; therefore I prefer this method of offering my good wishes and duty to my father and you. I shall carry this business through with the best of my abilities. The rest you know, is in the hands of Providence, to whose care I hope your good life and conduct will recommend your son . . . I heartily wish you health and enjoyment of the many good things that have fallen to your share. My best duty to the General.

I am, dear Madam,

Your obedient and affectionate son,

JAM; WOLFE

He took with him on *The Neptune* a miniature portrait of Katherine, whom in his correspondence he greets as his lover and implies a betrothal that was none the less left unannounced and unofficial. To his Uncle Walter in Dublin (yet another military Wolfe) he confided his plan both to marry and to leave the service if the weakness of his constitution allowed him to see his commission through to a victorious conclusion. He also had with him Katherine's copy of Gray's 'Elegy in a Country Churchyard' which he annotated heavily during the long, miserable, nauseating voyage. It was this poem, lugubriously beautiful in its metre and metaphor, and universally admired by Wolfe's generation, that gave rise to the most famous piece of Wolfiana: that on the eve of battle the General recited it to his soldiers. If in fact he did (and the sources are strong enough to resist the automatic modern assumption of apocrypha), it could hardly have raised their spirits even if it moved their souls, concluding as it did with the prophecy that *'the paths of glory lead but to the grave.'* 'I can only say, Gentlemen,' he is reported to have declared at its end, ' that if the choice were mine I would rather be the author of those verses than win the battle which we are to fight tomorrow morning.'

But Wolfe was always more than a waver of flags and a rattler of sabres. His driven, febrile personality, swinging between tender compassion and angry vanity, was haunted by Night Thoughts, by ravens perched on tombstones. If he was an empire-builder he knew he was also a grave-digger, perhaps his own. When he was feeling most embattled on the St. Lawrence, the news came to him of his father's death. This was not a shock since, as he had written to Uncle Walter, 'I left him in so weak a condition that it was not probable we should meet again'. But Wolfe's foreknowledge makes the chilling circumstances of his departure from England even more depressing. The 'general tenor' of his father's life, he wrote, 'has been extremely upright [so that] benevolent and little feelings of imperfections were overbalanced by his many good qualities.' Having delivered himself of this overly judicious obituary Wolfe betrayed a pathetic solitude; he was increasingly convinced that, whether by fire or fever, he would not survive to become a husband. 'I know you cannot cure my complaint,' he told his surgeon, 'but patch me up so I may be able to do my duty for the next few days and I shall be content.' His will dictated to his aides-de-camp shortly before the decisive battle asked for Katherine's portrait to be set with five hundred guineas worth of jewels and then returned to her.

To the elegiac resignation of Gray, Wolfe may have added his own Augustan conception of the Hero. For he also transcribed lines from Pope's translation of the *Iliad* together with his own inelegant but telling alterations:

> *But since, alas! ignoble age must come*
> *Disease and death's inexorable doom,*
> *The life which others pay, let us bestow,*
> *And give to Fame what we to Nature owe*
> *Brave let us fall or honoured if we live*
> *Or let us glory gain or glory give . . .*

The night came; the flotilla set off. Challenged with a '*Qui vive?*' the French-speaking Scot obliged with '*La France*', and persuaded the guards stationed above the river that they were a provisions fleet. '*Laissez les passer*', came the reassuring response. A gentle September breeze got up, rippling the water as the boats drifted along the high banks lined with walls of fir trees pointing at the stars. In the early hours, at their station, men were dropped into the landing boats which drifted back on the ebb; Wolfe sat bolt upright in one of them, anxious lest they overshoot their mark, which they duly did. So be it. It had to be this or nothing. He held in his hands the design of his posterity. By making Britain's history he could at last make his own. He was at the cliff face.

2. In Command

The Royal Academy Exhibition Gallery, Pall Mall, 29 April 1771.

It was the light that did the trick; a clean, shrewdly directed radiance illuminating the face of the martyr and bathing the grieving expressions of his brother officers in a reflection of impossible holiness. Benjamin West picked up this piece of artfulness from the stage (along with his device of arranging spectators on a platform projecting through the picture space as though it were a proscenium). In the theatre, candle-footlights or a hooped chandelier would highlight action on centre-stage against a background of carefully darkened obscurity from which characters would emerge or dissolve. West went one better by tearing back a patch of black cloud to expose a space of cerulean, celestial blue sky through which the sun shone; a light of sacred purity that seemed to embrace the expiring Hero. It was a stupendous piece of drama: brilliance and gloom, victory and death, saintly sacrifice and inconsolable sorrow set side by side, the sunlit sky of the imperial future banishing the grim clouds of past dissatisfactions. The public adored grandstanding performances and responded to this one with rapture. Asked by a spectator whether the painter had correctly caught the expression of a dying man, David Garrick was said to have thrown himself on the floor in the appropriate posture. The gallery rang with applause.

On 29 April 1771, the *Gentleman's Magazine* reported that an earthquake had struck Abingdon, Berkshire. Though but a moment's duration, it had lifted men and women off the ground while they were in their chairs. Others had felt the pavement sway and pitch. Something of the same sense of elation and terror, shock and anguish were experienced by the crowds at Pall Mall on the morning when West's painting, famous in rumour even before its exhibition, was at last exhibited. Lines had formed down the street for admission to the Royal Academy's galleries. A great deal of porter got drunk, a great many of Tiddy Dol's pies gnawed on to appease the growing impatience. Only the spectacle of so many high personages entering before the others offered some diversion. The crowd saw come and go: Lord Temple, William Pitt (now Lord

Benjamin West, *The Death of General Wolfe* (1770).

Chatham), ancient and tottering on his bandaged legs and crutches. He was later said to have spent much time before the painting, but to have complained about the general dejection to which the principals seemed (not surprisingly) to have succumbed. The famous and notorious beauty Georgiana, the Duchess of Devonshire, who had sketched Wolfe herself, came and went as conspicuously as possible; Horace Walpole offered predictably faint praise. The unimaginably wealthy Lord Richard Grosvenor attended; he had bought the painting for the outrageous sum of 400 guineas and many thought it had been commissioned for him in the first place. Finally the King arrived, and he had let it be known in advance that he did not want it.

George III, unlike his father, alongside whom Wolfe had fought at Dettingen, displayed a taste in painting that belied his reputation for bucolic simplicity. He was in fact the most sophisticated royal collector since Charles I (whom he much admired in other, not altogether agreeable, respects). His patronage, bestowed on the young and relatively obscure American artist five years earlier, had abruptly propelled West to celebrity and fortune. The King had heard something from his agents in Rome of a Pennsylvanian prodigy who was studying there at the time of his accession, assiduously copying Antique sculpture and the Renaissance masters. But it had been West's first serious sponsor and patron, William Drummond the Archbishop of York, who had brought him directly to the King's attention. The cleric had shown the King West's *Agrippina with the Ashes of Germanicus at Brundisium*, where a heroic procession files before the viewer on a shallow stage. In the background the action dimly unfolds while in the near foreground spectators turn towards the principals in rapt attention. It was the kind of thing the King liked: a history play in dignified motion, full of uplifting emotions and virtuous allusions but free of gimcrack mummery or Popish obscurantism. It was, in short, that thing for which the polite nation had been yearning: a British history painting.

On the strength of the *Agrippina* West was commissioned to do a second history, similar in format and expressly for George III. The subject was to be the Roman general Regulus, departing from his native city to return to Carthage. He had been captured in the Punic

Wars and allowed to return home to help sue for peace. Once there, however, his patriotic obligation required him to speak the truth and counsel against such an ignominious settlement of wrongs. Despite the certain knowledge that he would be put to death for his failure, his sense of honour obliged him to return to his captors. By repeating all the ingredients of the *Agrippina* West guaranteed that the King would be delighted, and so he was. When he learned, however, that his favourite painter was now contemplating a *Death of Wolfe* in which the figures were to be costumed in modern dress rather than the togas or chitons of the ancients, he let his dismay and displeasure be known.

There was another critic, whose authority had the power to do almost as much damage to West's career as the King's. In the same year that the American was working on the project that would surely make or break his reputation, Joshua Reynolds became *Sir Joshua Reynolds*. The honour was in recognition of his appointment as first President of the Royal Academy, itself only established in 1768. Reynolds was at the height of his powers, both as a virtuoso painter of portraits and histories and a theorist who in his work had redefined the canons of classicism. His *Discourses*, first set out as annual addresses to the Fellows and students of the Academy, aimed to establish universal criteria for the conjunction of Truth and Beauty, embodied first in antiquity and set, eternally, as the goals to which all high and polite art must unswervingly aim.

Though they were perhaps a little enamoured of visual anecdote and a little more theatrical than Reynolds would have liked, there was nothing hitherto in West's histories to occasion serious objection. On the strength of the works exhibited at Spring Gardens and, more importantly, of the King's favour, the American had in fact become an Academician. But reports of West's intentions to present Wolfe's death in contemporary dress struck Reynolds as an act of appalling vulgarity. John Galt, who wrote the first biography of West in the 1820s, made the story of Reynolds's and West's encounter famous. No doubt (since Galt wrote in accordance with West's elaborate wishes) it gives a more heroic account of the artist's uncompromising determination than may have actually been the case. Although self-serving and embellished it none the less gets the argument about making histories exactly right.

Reynolds's objection was not simply the stuffy complaint that West was violating convention. It was rather that by reporting naturalistically on a modern event he was robbing a history of the universal significance which its narrative ought to embody. If the history were to persuade and endure, it was imperative to find an idealized, universal language in which its exalted conceptions could be represented, and not to distract the beholder with a flashy and elaborate spectacle, heavy with 'minute particularities of dress'. West's response, as reported by Galt, was famously and invincibly American.

> 'I began by remarking that the event intended to be commemorated took place on the 13th of September 1758 [a year off!] in a region of the world unknown to the Greeks and Romans and at a period of time when no such nation and heroes in their costume any longer existed. The subject I have to represent is the conquest of a great province of America by the British troops. It is a topic that history will proudly record and the same truth that guides the pen of the historian should govern the pencil of the artist . . . '

Disarmingly straightforward though West's reply was, in one respect it was disingenuous. For in a different voice (more authentically his own) he made the opposite point, perhaps much closer to his personal truth, that the painter's history and the writer's were in fact not in the least analogous; that he was the master of one skill and a hobbling cripple in the other. In a letter to his cousin, Peter Thomson, he apologized for not having written sooner, but the truth of the matter was:

> 'I don't like writeing—its as difficult for me as painting would be to you—every man in his way, I could soon as paint you a description of things on this side of the water . . . I believe I should have made a figure in South America in the time of the conquest when we find the natives of that country communicated with each other by painting the Images of their Amaginations & not in writeing characters to describe them . . . [but since] how

writeing is your profession [Thomson was a conveyancer] it will make me happy in now and then receiving a specimen of your great abilities in that way & I will promise you for the future I will endeavour to answer them in either Painting or Scrawling.'

For all his formal protestations, then, West was not a reporter in paint; a writer of historical prose. He was a poetic inventor. He was artful in constructing an image of himself as the unspoiled colonial; intuitive, doggedly empirical, an innocent abroad, since so much of polite London found the image beguiling. In fact his deviation from the conventions of academic history painting rested on more subtle grounds. He had exposed a serious contradiction in its requirements—both to be strictly faithful to the details to narrative *and* to render them poetically noble by the exercise of the imagination. Through the breach in these incompatible demands, West drove his mighty, painterly, coach and four. The result was *The Death of Wolfe*, his masterpiece.

From its first conception, West rejected literalism and embraced rhetoric. 'Wolfe must not die like a common soldier under a Bush,' he wrote. 'To move the mind there should be a spectacle presented to raise and warm the mind and all should be proportiond to the highest idea conceivd of the Hero . . . A mere matter of fact will never produce the effect.' Accordingly, throughout the composition, from top to bottom, mere fact is overwhelmed by inspired, symbolically loaded invention. It was this unapologetic hyperbole which set West's painting off so dramatically from the prosaic versions that preceded it, none more painfully feeble than Edward Penny's effort of 1763. Where that product of honest toil conscientiously had the General attended only by two officers and set down in a shrubby clearing apart from the battlefield, West produced the grandiloquent lie the public craved: a death at the very centre of the action; with the firing of guns still sounding at his back; the St. Lawrence that he had finally conquered to his right, three groups of officers and men arrayed like a Greek chorus to witness the tragedy.

Of the *dramatis personae* only Monckton, standing at the left,

Edward Penny, *The Death of General Wolfe* (1763), detail.

Isaac Barré, leaning over the General from behind, and Hervey Smyth, his aide-de-camp, holding his arm on the left, had played conspicuous parts on the Heights of Abraham. But Monckton, himself badly wounded, was busy in another part of the field at the time of Wolfe's death. Apparently there was a surgeon brought to help stanch Wolfe's three wounds but it was certainly not the mysterious 'Adair' identified as the figure at his right. Nor was the Ranger at the left Captain Howe (of later fame in the American war). But the most startling fiction of all was the Indian, posed in the antique form of poetic contemplation, precisely the quality commonly denied to the 'savages' as they were invariably called by the British of Wolfe's generation. The General himself had considered them to be irredeemable barbarians, cruel and depraved. What is more they fought, exclusively, for the other side. In fact, it seems likely that the Indian auxiliaries of the French, concealed in the long grass and corn and picking off individual British soldiers, did more damage to Wolfe's troops than the French regulars. The bizarre notion that Wolfe would have tolerated their presence at the moment of his apotheosis would have been a bitter jest to anyone familiar with his prejudices.

West's sentiments, on the other hand, were quite different. He had seen the Mohawks employed not as enemies but allies of the British in Pennsylvania, and had idealized them as the embodiments of native nobility. His generation and Wolfe's were separated less by a great span of years than by an immense gap in taste. What the Augustans saw as repellent barbarity, the devotees of *sensibility* thought virile, natural and uncorrupted. West had already painted a genre scene of a Mohawk family and in his history of Penn's Treaty with the Indians would reiterate this essentially benign view of the relations between the races. So if Wolfe's death were to be designed as a tragic history of antique grandeur, how better to reinforce it than by making the Indian embody the essence of natural aristocracy in his Michelangelesque torso and noble, even Roman, profile?

There was another reason for the inclusion of these figures at the left: they were there to celebrate America itself; the raw vigour of the New World, a place of buckskin and forest virtues that might supply the necessary power and resources to regenerate a decadent and enervated Europe. Just as the great towering flag of the Union proclaimed the might of the British empire, the Ranger and the Indian announced (prematurely) its essentially American identity. Together these morally charged insignia turned West's painting into a secular Passion scene, a Lamentation, an icon of the British Empire.

It was, however, an icon that told a story. West borrowed heavily from stage drama (as well as traditional history paintings) to transpose a narrative sequence to the frieze of figures lined up parallel to the picture plane. The eye is meant to read mid- and background action right to left, beginning with the elements that made the battle possible—the British fleet anchored on the river, then the action of the dawn of 13 September with field-guns being hauled into place. At the extreme left West records the decisive turning-point of the battle when the British infantry unloosed the devastating musket volley on the confident, advancing French. From this point the eye turns and travels in the reverse direction left to right, moving with the messenger who brings news of the victory (a figure whom West brought closer and closer to the scene of the central group as he made further copies on commission). The waving hat of the messenger connects with the pointing hand of the Ranger in whose mouth the public, well-versed in Wolfiana, would put the words 'They run,' said to have been reported to the dying commander. The sash supporting Monckton's wound runs parallel to his left arm, which in turn drops significantly in the direction of Wolfe's own wrist, shattered by the first hit he had taken. On his face with the eyes rolled upwards both in a death agony and the traditional expression of beatific ecstasy, the lips part to utter the lines which in many reported variations thanked God for the news of the victory. Finally, as a kind of dramatic post mortem the two unidentified soldiers on the extreme right act as mourners with hands clasped and eyes lowered in expressions of reverent prayer.

West also pulled together groups of figures with almost symphonic power and articulation. He confined the background action of the battle to a great diagonal wedge, dimly lit except at the horizon, where a brilliant streak of light hovers above the British ships, their masts puncturing the skyline. The foreground figures are set in three distinct triangular groups, yet they are all enclosed within a larger triangle that has the point of the British flag at its apex and the fallen emblems of the imperial war—Grenadier's hat; Wolfe's musket—running along its base. At the centre of this great mass of forms lie two crucially connected spaces: Wolfe's body contained in a slumping parallelogram or ellipse, and the flag, exactly aligned with it, the billowing fold emphasized by the chiaroscuro of the clouds. The banner thus becomes Wolfe's cross; his saintly attribute; the shroud for his body and the meaning of his history.

It was a stunning *tour de force* that, in public opinion, all but annihilated the reservations of the dwindling band of critics. The King was sufficiently moved from his initial scepticism to commission a copy from West, who subsequently painted another four for various patrons. For those beyond London and even beyond England who were unable to see the painting, the publisher and cultural entrepreneur Richard Boydell had William Woollett engrave the painting. Though it was an expensive print—perhaps five guineas—the engraving sold in phenomenal quantities. Boydell made his fortune from this single work, netting what, for the eighteenth century, was the staggering sum of £15,000. He went on to become an Alderman of the City of London and the publisher of the Shakespeare Gallery, the city's most powerful cultural entrepreneur. Woollett seems to have been the first engraver to be paid on a royalty basis, so that he too became rich on the back of West's genius to the tune of £7,000.

As for Benjamin West himself, no less than his subject, he had climbed to the summit of his powers and reputation. He was officially designated court history painter to the King and produced another fifty paintings for the avid George III. But none of them remotely approached the dramatic intensity and sweep of the *Wolfe*. Since one death scene had worked so well (and since the deathbed was a favourite spectacle of late eighteenth-century taste) he tried many more, each feebler than the last. The *Death of Bayard* was a little better than the *Death of Epaminondas*, which in turn was much better than his unfinished and oddly reticent *Death of Chatham*, until at last the genre completely collapsed along with its subject in the histrionic failure of the *Death of Nelson*.

It seems likely, though, that this affable and harmlessly

Benjamin West, *The Death of the Earl of Chatham* (above) and *The Death of Nelson.*

conceited man was content enough with his status and wealth not to fret unduly over the fading powers of the Muse. Comfortably ensconced in Panton Square with his wife Betsey and their children, he wrote cheerfully in his atrocious syntax and spelling:

> 'I can say I have been so fare successful in that I find my pictures sell for a prise that no living artist ever received before. I hope this is a circumstance that will induce others to do the same for the great necessity a man is under to have money in his Pokt often distracts the studies of youths contreary to theitr geniuses.'

Notwithstanding Reynolds's objections, West remained a pillar of the Academy and in 1795 had the rich satisfaction of actually succeeding his old critic in the Presidential chair.

What had he done to Wolfe, his memory, his history? The success of the painting, in all its fanciful inventions and excesses of poetic licence, had been such that when British children of future generations grew up drilled in the pieties of imperial history, it was West's scene they imagined rather than any more literal account. Art had entirely blotted out mere recall, let alone evidence. Two years after the exhibition on the Pall Mall, the marble monument to Wolfe, commissioned as early as 1759, was finally unveiled in Westminster Abbey. The sculptor, Wilton, had also managed to combine allegory and history by having a decorously half-draped Wolfe attended by two officers in contemporary dress, while Fame brings the obligatory laurels and the battle is recorded on bas-relief below. In its genre the monument is an unexceptional and sentimental tribute, and with West's rhetoric imprinted in the popular mind it never manages to become more than a footnote to his achievement.

After West, nothing could dispel the odour of sanctity that lay over Wolfe's memory. When George Townshend published a mordant satire on the monument project around the theme of the Vanity of Human Glory, the Duke of Albermarle was so incensed that he challenged him to a duel, and was prevailed on to desist only by the personal intervention of Pitt. And while the stars of other imperial conquistadors—Robert Clive, Warren Hastings—fell almost as precipitously as they had risen, Wolfe's remained sempiternally brilliant.

What more could possibly be said?

Benjamin West, *Self-Portrait* (circa 1770).

3. Deep in the Forest

The Massachusetts Historical Society, 21 November 1893.

It was not quite Thanksgiving. Dead leaves, brown and papery, piled up against the curbstones; a grey November light mantled red-brick Boston and forty sombre men filed into the meeting room of the Massachusetts Historical Society on Boylston Street. It was one of those morally upholstered places where the Boston Brahmins could defeat the contradictions of their Puritan legacy by feeling dignified and comfortable at the same time. A whole day, carefully planned, could be spent moving from one such *sanctum* to the next: the Athenaeum for the morning, the Botolph Club for lunch; the Society for the afternoon. The agreeable consequence was that a Brahmin backside would be welcomed only by studded leather armchairs; a Brahmin sensibility soothed by oak-panelled walls and unassertive, familiar company; the Brahmin temper left undisturbed to read, snore or sniff a weak brandy and water. Thus sheltered from the incivilities of modern life, the barbarian hordes—plutocrats, democrats, Jews in West Roxbury, Irish in south Boston, women, loquacious, determined, vexing women— might all be safely relegated to the remote horizons of the next century.

For the time being, at least, history if not wholly on their side was at least firmly in their custody. And they had come, this bleak afternoon, to pay tribute to one of the pillars of their temple, now fallen; by common consent, the greatest and the oddest of their company—Francis Parkman. There were ancestral names among them, keepers of the flame, a true priesthood amidst the hard paganism of the modern time: Adamses and Coolidges, Winthrops and Lowells; and only his own manifold infirmities had kept Leverett Saltonstall away. Compared with these tribes of the righteous, the Parkmans had been nothing much—a mercantile fortune; a succession of inevitable Unitarian preachers leavened with the occasional family ne'er-do-well. But Parkman himself had become one of their number as surely as if to the manner born: a Harvard Overseer; the first President of the Botolph; a gentleman scholar, rose-grower and anti-feminist; a man whose whole life had been consumed by the historical vocation; in short, one of nature's aristocrats.

His death, at the beginning of the month, in his seventieth year, could hardly have taken the members of the Society by surprise. Parkman had been crippled with arthritis and rheumatism, smitten with failing sight; his strength seemed to have ebbed lately and he had stayed put for the summer at his cottage on Jamaica Pond. Some privately marvelled that with all his sicknesses, he had survived to his three score and ten and attributed this to an iron determination to complete his great epic of France and England's struggle in North America. But as obvious as Parkman's ill health had been, they had long been accustomed to his figure, upright in the invalid chair, wheeling about the parlours of Boston. Indeed he had been ill so long, death almost seemed an illogical interruption. So when President Ellis had announced his passing at their regular meeting on 3 November, there were many who felt the news with an unexpectedly keen sorrow. Worse, they had to sit through Charles Adams's lengthy report on his experience of the Chicago World's Fair, a phenomenon that Parkman could reliably have been expected to have detested. To general amazement Adams, who like all his family was hard to please, seemed to have been quite taken with the whole thing. There had been, he claimed, a gratifying 'spirit of order and decorum . . . a noticeable absence of rudeness or scolding and absolutely no loud language or profanity much less roughness or violence.' Even the Babylonian scale of the expense—a shocking thirty million dollars—failed to dim Adams's unseemly exhilaration. 'Of all the visions of architectural beauty which human eyes have dwelt upon, it may well be asked if anything can compare or, even approached the Chicago Fair.'

It was fitting, then, that a Special Meeting should have been called (as President Ellis noted the event, exceptional in the Society's hundred-year history) to be dedicated to Parkman's memory. They could expect (and duly got) some funeral verses from Oliver Wendell Holmes: '*He rests from toil; the portals of the tomb/Close on the last of those unwearying hands/That wove their pictured webs.*' Members distinguished in historical letters would, in all likelihood, place their own prosy wreaths on his bier. But there was to be something more; something they might anticipate with great curiosity, even excitement. Ellis had let it be known that many years before, in 1868, Parkman had confided an autobiographical memoir to his friend, to be read to the Society only after his death. Now the moment had come when this might be shared with his colleagues. Perhaps it would disclose the mysteries of Parkman's prodigious craft; his gift of painting in paragraphs, of recreating the identities of La Salle and Champlain, Montcalm and Wolfe, of tracking their destinies through the forests and river valleys of pristine North America, of giving meaning to their lives and their deaths. Perhaps they would learn how he had made history.

To begin with, there was a charmingly self-deprecating preface, evidently added when Parkman had reviewed the memoir. 'Running my eye over this paper,' he had written, 'I am more than ever struck with its *egoism* which makes it totally unfit for any eye but that of one in close personal relations with me.' 'No, no,' came the muffled politenesses in response and in any event Ellis proceeded. But as he did, it became suddenly, dismayingly apparent that the document *was* indeed saturated, even supersaturated with egoism, not in the least diminished (in fact reinforced) by Parkman's manner of referring to himself in the third person. Moreover, what they were listening to, with rapidly mounting discomfort, was not history at all but case history. It spoke to them of sickness, torments mental and physical, an unceasing, unsparing war between body and mind; of monstrously self-imposed ordeals, and despair at imagined imperfections. They had known a man who (in all but his work) seemed to them the very epitome of Yankee resilience, stoicism and intellectual toughness. What fell from these pages was the self-portrait of a creature in pain. The great engine of historical creation they had so admired was, he now confessed, a machine horribly out of control, 'a locomotive, built of indifferent material under a head of steam too great for its strength, hissing at a score of crevices yet rushing on at accelerating speed to the inevitable smash.'

Was he, then, a Samson Agonistes, whom they had imagined an American Thucydides? Was this poor tragic figure, crumpled in pain and hysteria, the same man whose prose had encompassed the American landscape and had made of the death of Wolfe a great transfiguration? Was this truly Parkman, the historian-as-hero?

50 Chestnut Street, Boston, February 1880.

It was all the wrong way about. When there was darkness in the streets of Beacon Hill, his brain flooded with light; that brilliant needle-sharp light of the plains; the light that kept him writhing with insomnia. When there was daylight, he had to fortify his north-facing study at the top of the house, to keep it away. On mercifully grey mornings he could open the shutters a little but when a hard winter sun shone, the dry radiance irritated his cornea and flooded his eyes with tears. Then there was nothing for it but to close the heavy drapes altogether, and work by candle-light. If he then shut his eyes he could listen more attentively, as the girl read documents to him in her fractured Boston-Irish French, comprehending nothing of what she said. Only in his blackness could he make those words live; people his imagination and the Canadian landscape with soldiers and forts, Indians and creaking boats; inscribe into his chronicle utterances and acts, decisions and their consequences. His wisdom had turned owlish; his history nocturnal; his strength rose when others slept.

There were times, now, when he could, if he was very careful, manage a little reading himself; five or ten minutes at a time, followed by as many minutes again of rest. In this way he could, on his best days, his hand shading his brow, complete a whole morning of such staccato work. But there were times too when he overdid it and would collapse into such terrible pain and exhaustion that the Bigelow sisters would have to nurse him back with thin soup and tepid tea. If he avoided these crises it might even be possible to write directly, rather than dictate. He worked with red pencil on orange paper—the combination of colours that seemed least glaring—in a neat, economical hand. But there would be days when his mind was steeled for the exercise but his body conspired against it; when arthritis made it impossible to bend his forearm. On such days he might bring out a contraption he devised twenty years before to cope with his failing sight. Wires guided his hand across the horizontal lines so that he might actually write with his eyes shut. But the wooden frame to which they were attached could also be stood on end, like a small music stand or artist's pad, so that he might work with an arm extended in the manner of a painter.

By such fits and starts; with interruptions and withdrawals, his great chronicle of the encounter of France and England in North America grew, chapter by chapter, volume by volume. His ailments made it an inconceivably laborious process and his working convictions made it more so. For Francis Parkman refused the short-cuts offered by secondary sources, almost all of which he despised, being the pompous adjudications of dull men on other dull men; the 'pallid and emasculate scholarship' of which he so often complained. Instead he worked only with primary materials—crates of letters and journals; account books and ordinances—that he had found on his travels in France and England or which his long-suffering friend the good Père Casgrain sent him. Batches of these, organized by chronology and theme, would be read to him over and again until from their scraps and shreds he had sewn together in his mind the splendid fabric of his history. Was there any historian before him, he wondered, who could so well understand the meaning of the word painstaking?

The history of this history began long before its writing. For Parkman it had started in childhood, just as Wolfe had accepted his destiny as a soldier's son and a mother's hero. Parkman rebelled against the expectations of his parents against the suffocating reasonableness of their Unitarianism, the mercantile urbanity they and their kind prized. When early signs of a 'fragile constitution' had indicated therapeutic exposure to fresh air, Francis Parkman Sr. had packed the boy off to his uncle's farm at Medford. From there he had gone roaming in the Fells, wandering into the thick woods of cedars, red oaks and pines, trapping squirrel and chasing woodchuck from their burrows. He was already in search of a pristine America; one not so old perhaps as the pitted red volcanic rock over which he clambered, but an arboreal, wild place of freedom and purity. He could feel it in the springy rug of leaf and moss, smell it in the savoury mould of its generations and regenerations. It was then, he recollected, that he had first imagined writing an American history that would have the forest as its principal character. Later (but not much) he thought the 'Old War' of 1756-63, whose history had been blotted out by the self-congratulatory brilliance of the Revolution, might be just such an heroic enterprise. It was, after all, a story that turned on the moment when one kind of world, a culture driven by faith and authority but damaged by dogma and subservience, would be confronted by another whose energies sprang from aggressive, unruly improvisation. France and England, trappers and priests, soldiers and marines, commanders and intendants, bound together in combat, seemed to him material at least as epic as anything recorded in the annals of Greece and Rome. The climax of their encounter, on the Heights of Abraham, was, he imagined, one of those moments in which a whole universe now remote in its values and virtues was reformed into the shape required by modern empires. Wolfe and Montcalm were, then, chivalric figures; incarnations of duty, sacrifice and resolution; doomed, both victor and vanquished, to perish before a world which had brushed those fancies aside.

What was wanting for such a history, Parkman was further convinced, as he sat in Harvard Hall, captive to the interminable lectures of Jared Sparks, was a new voice. It had to be unapologetically American; a voice liberated from the muffled formalism of the British tradition. What could such people, who dwelled amidst fog and soot, and whose apprehension of the sublime was limited by landscapes of rolling hills and grassy vales, what could they know of the forest; of river valleys that cut through gorges atop which immense conifers towered and leaned, enclosing things within their density which Shropshire and Wiltshire could never fathom. Those English voices that sang most sweetly to his ear—Milton and Byron—were lyric, free of the laconic politeness that had so enfeebled the language. Like others of his generation who turned against their Unitarian fathers—Longfellow and Whitman—Parkman too wished to give lyric expression to his exhilaration with the landscape and history, the space and time, of his nation.

To find such eloquence, he already knew, would not be easy. There remained in him enough of his Puritan forefathers to believe that it must be earned through grinding labour and ordeal. Nor would he find what he sought in the library or even the archive, places where the spirit became desiccated. It awaited him somewhere beyond the academy; in the landscape itself.

So his education as a young man filled the spaces where Harvard was not. On every vacation he took himself off with a few companions, sometimes without company, on long, punishing walking expeditions in New Hampshire and Maine; to Lake George and the Notch. In silent river valleys and lakeside clearings he communed with ghostly figures whose hatchets had already cut a path but who had left no tracks and no history other than the rudimentary jottings of a journal; perfunctory lines in a sketch-book. Parkman planned his journeys precisely to recover as far as he could the direct, physical experience of those whose lives he would one day write: spoke to ancient survivors of the Revolutionary war; hunted and pitched tent where he knew the Canadian Jesuits, where trappers and their Indian allies, had stayed; marched along the paths taken by British soldiers toward hapless ambush or brilliant victory.

Sometimes this naïve passion for authenticity, the need to hear a twig break beneath his foot as it had for Champlain or Howe, led him directly to disaster. In his wanderings he fell from sheer cliff paths; sank to his chest in swamp; was eaten alive by clouds of ravenous blackfly and pitched from his flimsy canoe into the bone-chilling waters of the Magalloway. His body began to record these histories in scars, dislocations, dull muscular aches that in later life would cripple legs and arms.

But Parkman's demanding muse remained undeterred. If anything, like the Jesuit fathers whose tenacity he would chronicle with grudging respect, his sense of mission fed on these bruising adversities. Not that he seemed unhappy or solitary at Harvard. Quite the contrary, he had something of a reputation for gregariousness: a stalwart of the Hasty Pudding and the Chit-Chat Club. Yet, something was longing to break free of undergraduate affability. In 1843, in his junior year, he plunged into a black depression; explained (as many times afterwards) by the punishments of his physical routines and by bizarre references to chemistry experiments in his youth that he genuinely believed had introduced something unwholesome into his metabolism.

Therapy for his sinister and baffling contamination, as for all young men of his rank and culture, was Europe. But Parkman let it be known that he wanted to avoid the standard route of the Grand Tour, and his writings are full of bored contempt for temples classical and Christian. Instead he opted for what was fast becoming the alternative Tour of the Romantic generation— Sicily and Naples, rather than Florence and Rome; the rugged extremities of the country rather than the cultivated centre. In Sicily the young Bostonian drank deep of the 'black Falernian wine' and made the obligatory Gothic pilgrimage to the Palermo catacombs. Pushing his way through crowds of beggars, whores and the great tribes of cats (that were, at least, preferable to the rats they were kept to deal with) Parkman descended into the black depths. 'Mummies, each from his niche in the wall grinned at us diabolically . . . Coffins piled up below, men—shrunk to a mere nothing, but clothed as they used to be above ground . . . a row of skulls under the cornices . . . ' This was not, he thought, any kind of communing with lost souls; rather an indulgence in the grotesque; a costumed trash collection of the defunct: 'children just dead', a few men flung down in a 'corner awaiting the drying up process'.

He needed other kinds of company. In Rome he oscillated between excesses of sybaritic abandonment (as much as a Yankee could) and excesses of organized self-mortification. The carnival gave him the first; a monastery of the hair-shirted Order of the Passionists, a punishing dose of the latter. In the deafening, dancing tumult of the carnival Parkman drowned in wine and flowers and became excited as he pelted unattainable women with roses.

> 'To battle with flowers against a laughing and conscious face—showering your ammunition thick as the carriage passes the balcony then straining your eyes to catch the last glance of the blackeyed witch and the last wave of the hand as the crowd closes around her, this is no contemptible amusement. . . '

Aroused by heat and turmoil, Parkman none the less remained in thrall to his obsession with America's chilly wildness. As stunning a spectacle as Lake Como, glistening below the Alps, merely ended up reminding him that it was a pale reflection of the unkempt glories of Lake George. Metropolitan Europe was worse. Paris and London, the one devoted to pleasure, the other to commerce, reinforced his prejudice that the great cities were places of moral contamination, full of human types whose degeneracy was of a piece with their habitat. In London he went out of his way to harass 'some wretched clerk' whose 'vacant lobster eyes, nose elevated in the air and elbows stuck out at right angles, a pewter knob of a cane playing at his lip' marked him out as a quarry for the American hunter. Following closely on his heels he frightened the creature into supposing he was being pursued by a criminal, and was then vastly amused by his victim's discomfort.

Evidently Parkman was not, as his parents imagined, destined to be a lawyer. He had another apprenticeship altogether in mind. Between lectures at Harvard Law School he took lessons in bareback riding from a company of circus riders then in Cambridge. This was to give him the skills he imagined he would need on an expedition to the West, following the routes of the wagon trains. There on the prairies he might find his starting point, a world of Indian and buffalo: primitive America, the place from which his histories, wherever they might lead, had to begin.

In the spring of 1846 Parkman set off with one of his Harvard friends and a kinsman whose very name proclaimed his pedigree: Quincy Adams Shaw. From Ohio they went by steamboat to the 'jump-off' at St. Louis. In the beginning Parkman rejoiced, much as he had in Sicily, at his release from the starchy civilities of Atlantic culture. But it was not long before all his imagined epiphany with the West decomposed under a brutal sun and the terrifying illimitable space of the prairie. Instead of feeling married to the landscape, much of it repelled and threatened him. The heat was 'sultry and almost insupportable'; the immense electrical storms rolling around and around the horizon, horrid, fearsome things; the noble buffalo (when finally sighted) 'no very attractive spectacle with their shaggy manes and the tattered remnants of last winter covering their backs in irregular shreds and patches and flying off as they ran'; the cacti hung 'like reptiles at the edge of every ravine'. The human specimens were not much better, pelt traders living in tents slung with grimy hides, with bloated squaws for company, one memorably described by Parkman as an 'impersonation of gluttony and laziness' hidden deep in the recesses of her tepee. Indeed the Plains Indians, so far from embodying the qualities of a natural aristocracy or resisting the arrogant and corrupting intrusions of the average American, appeared to Parkman to display most of the wretchedness of the whites in even more squalid and incorrigible style. Pawnees hated Crow who mistrusted the Dakota who preyed on the Arapahoe. It was nothing but an endless scavenger hunt in a Godforsaken desert.

It was finished before it had begun, then, this romance with the West. He had thought to find some sort of wellspring for America and had discovered instead a barren thing; an antechamber, not of heaven, but of hell. The force of the disenchantment nearly killed him. As the members of the Massachusetts Historical Society heard the memoir reach the Oregon Trail, they listened to a self-portrait of pathetic horror; a man humiliated by incapacity; half-dead with sickness, eaten up with remorse, 'reeling in the saddle with weakness and pain'. The sun, he thought, had blinded him; his stomach heaved and gagged; his brow dripped with fever. Between a constantly disappearing Valhalla on the western horizon and a retreat back east he was lost, paralysed. Of all the sketches in *The Oregon Trail* none so much resembles a self-portrait as the jetsam of discarded furniture he saw lying about the prairie trail: 'shattered wrecks of ancient clawfooted tables, well-waxed and rubbed or massive bureaus of oak.' These were fine great things that had migrated long ago from England, settled in New England, been transported to Ohio or Kentucky and then, under some delusion, dragged west before the 'cherished relic is . . . flung out to scorch and crack on the plains.'

Parkman returned in a state that swung crazily from manic compulsion to complete prostration. 'A wild whirl possessed his brain' (he wrote of himself at this time), joined to a universal turmoil of the nervous system which put his philosophy to the sharpest test it had hitherto known. He was incapable of writing up the Oregon Trail notes; it was done for him by his friends Shaw and Charles Eliot Norton, so that the finished result is even more sardonic, condescending and unsympathetic to the West than would have been the case had he finished it himself. A year later, in 1848,

Parkman none the less determined to begin writing history with an Indian chronicle—not that of the sorry remnant he had encountered but the last great defiance of Pontiac against Anglo-French manipulation. It would be a history where he could forget the nightmare of the open plain and take cover once more in the undergrowth and cool darkness of the conspiratorial woods. It would be the first chapter of the great epic of the forest.

The ten years that followed were the best and worst of his life; the beginnings of a creative outpouring. Real pain mixed with hysteria; neurasthenic obsession with hypochondria and insomnia. In the midst of a summer heat wave he thought empathetically of three toads in his garden at Jamaica Plain 'stewed to death under the stones where they ensconced themselves.' The family rallied round, did what they could to nurse him and protect him from himself; they were thinking of other black strains in the stock—Uncle George Parkman, whose real estate speculations were notoriously profitable and who had written extensively on the care of lunatics, had just recently been murdered by a debtor of his who also happened to be a Harvard Professor of Mineralogy. Though a legal opinion protested the conviction on the grounds of circumstantial evidence, parts of the body that had been discovered close to the Professor's laboratory in the Medical School (a building donated by Uncle George) had included false teeth identified as those of the victim.

Yet there was little on Francis Parkman's written pages to suggest a man stranded at the border of his sanity, in the grip of convulsions. Whether dictated or painfully pencilled along the wire guides of his writing frame, the end result was often expansive, thoughtful and elegant, and at times sardonic. Despite the periodic descents into anguish, writing *The Conspiracy of Pontiac* Parkman believed he had held at bay 'The Enemy', as he called the formless beast that stalked his footsteps in and out of the forest of his mind.

And when he felt The Enemy was closing in, there were fresh troops at hand to come to his rescue. In 1850 he met and married Catherine Scollay Bigelow, herself a product of two of Boston's most famous clans. The match could not have been more ideally suited to Parkman's peculiar needs for her father was a celebrated physician and she a devotee of the northern New England landscapes. It was ultimately on those cold hills and dense woods that the historian had set his sights; a sharp turn away from the western prairies and back to the theatre of the Anglo-French wars.

'His martial instincts were balanced by strong domestic inclinations,' Parkman would write of Wolfe, and as usual, they applied equally to himself. Agitated and insecure as he was, somehow Parkman constructed a kind of nest for himself (or rather had it built for him by the women of his family). After his father's death in 1852 they spent the bitter winters in town in the big brick house on Walnut Street and the summer in the leafy suburban village of Milton. In 1853 Francis Jr. was born and though now in the trough of a clinical depression, Parkman managed to rally enough to design and build a fair-season cottage at Jamaica Pond. This was to be the closest to a home that he ever experienced; three acres, a reedy, lily-strewn patch of water on which he rowed, his back to the sun.

The idyll quickly evaporated. In 1857 his four-year-old son died and although a daughter, Katherine, was born the same year, the birth did little to raise his wife from the depths of grief. She herself died in 1858, leaving a new baby, Mary, and her husband now completely lost in a great billowing tide of hysterical wretchedness.

The Enemy seemed to have triumphed after all. Picking up the pieces of this human wreckage, the Bigelows stepped in. Parkman's sisters-in-law came out to the cottage to nurse both father and children; then in the fall shipped them back to Chestnut Street, the house that became the historian's asylum from others and himself. Mother Harvard, in the guise of the Medical Faculty, stepped in to concern herself with the fate of this lost son. 'Displaying that exuberance of resource for which that remarkable profession is justly famed,' he later wrote in bitter reflection, '. . . one was for tonics, another for a diet of milk; one counselled galvanism, another hydropathy; one scarred him behind the neck with nitric acid, another drew red hot irons along his spine with a view of enlivening that organ . . . One assured him of recovery. Another, with grave circumlocution lest the patient should take fright, informed him he was the victim of an organic disease of the brain which must needs dispatch him to another world within twelve month . . . '

After a ghoulish winter in Paris in 1858, Parkman came back to the house on the pond. All he had done in the past decade was a feeble, self-indulgent romantic novel called *Vassall Morton*, but even this kind of creative power had left him in the years of total collapse. Yet groping through the jumbled sequence of darkness and light, there was something, at the end of it all, that beckoned him back to mental order. If almost all his faculties seemed to have defected to The Enemy—his sight, his capacity to walk or write—there was one at least that remained loyal, his sense of smell. Parkman's nose was, in fact, a mighty thing: bold and big-boned and powerfully fleshed-out. It could inhale the fragrance of flowers that must have bathed his distracted brain with pleasure. For *en route* to recovering his life as Parkman the Historian, he became Parkman the Horticulturalist, building first a greenhouse; then growing lilies and roses; then experimenting with new grafts and strains until, finally, he had created an entire realm of flowers. Perhaps he recalled that earlier carnival battle in Rome when he had hurled blooms at girls on balconies. As his horticulture flourished so life gradually returned. He published *The Book of Roses* in 1861; became more famous as a gardener than a historian; was appointed Professor of Horticulture at Harvard; and gradually, hesitantly, from his garden path, approached again the forbidding immensity of the woods.

And then, from the mid-1860s, he entered their history. The summers were usually given over to the world of the Pond; the winters in the study at Chestnut Street, to *France and England in North America*. Box after box of documents came from his archivist friends in Paris and Canada. Sometimes he felt strong enough to travel and gather his own documents that would be shipped back to Boston. The ponderous routine of being read to, of dictating, of having his own work read back and refined and edited, began. The Enemy now put in only an occasional appearance, usually during the long, merciless nights of his insomnia. But given a soft grey morning light and Parkman could proceed again, a few minutes at a time, to his business.

Francis Parkman in 1861.

Others were going blind in Boston in the service of Clio: Prescott, the great chronicler of the Conquests, most famously. But Parkman had evolved into a craftsman whose energies were pinpointed into minute detailed tasks. He had become a stitcher of tapestry, albeit with slowness, like those at Bayeux who had chronicled another encounter between France and England; Norman power and Saxon bloody-mindedness. Like such a tapestry, there were brilliantly fabricated moments, flights of pure fanciful embroidery, stitched into the epic. But when he and others could stand back and look at the thing, unfolding before them, the marvel of it all was unmistakable.

And now it was almost done. The previous summer he had gone to Quebec once more to see the grassy field at the Heights of Abraham; to stand at the face of the cliff and imagine again the daunting ascent; the sheer improbability of it. The time had come to deliver Wolfe to his consummation and Montcalm to his, surely a symmetry of providential design (however much his ingrown doubt rebelled against any such nonsense). Perhaps, though, all his own trials were in some measure a preparation that he could better understand the compulsive, perfervid intensity of the General. He wrote of Wolfe:

'When bound on some deadly enterprise of war he calmly counts whether or not he can compel his feeble body to bear him on till the work is done. A frame so delicately strung could not have been insensible to danger; but forgetfulness of self and the absorption of every faculty in the object before him, shut out the sense of fear . . . His nature was a combination of tenderness and fire . . . He made friends readily and kept them and was usually a pleasant companion though subject to sallies of imperious irritability which occasionally broke through his strong sense of good breeding. For this his susceptible constitution was largely answerable for he was a living barometer and his spirits rose and fell with every change of weather . . . '

At the supreme crisis of his life, with his army withering away, Wolfe

> '. . . lay in an upper chamber, helpless in bed, his singular and unmilitary features haggard with disease and drawn with pain, no man could less have looked the hero. But as the needle, though quivering, points always to the pole, so through torment and languor and the heats of fever the mind of Wolfe dwelt on the capture of Quebec . . .'

Past and present dissolved at this moment. He became Wolfe and Wolfe lived again through him; the man's perseverance and fortitude; the punishments of his body; the irritability of his mind; the crazy, agitated propulsion of his energies all flowed between subject and historian; overtook and consumed him, robbed him of sleep and colonized his days so that the writing of it all, the remembering, the recitation drove him on, relentlessly, became akin to and part of the hard, forced climb upwards to the heights; the drum-measured advance across the field, unstoppable till the very finish.

4. On the Heights of Abraham

Nine a.m., 13 September 1759.

An ill day for a battle we thought, hard to see our enemy with the wet mist hanging on the hill betwixt us and them and the rain falling. When the low sun appear'd it shone straight in our eyes as we faced the town where the French were musterd in front of the walls. So at the start we heard more than we saw, first their drums and the clatter of some pieces and the low sound of men beginning their march. The General knew we were as much afraid as any men in such a position, who could have no way back and were held from going forward, so he came along the line to us and spoke some words to help our resolve and keep us still until it was time to fire.

We were tried, God knows, for as they came closer, the first musket shots came, cracking and hissing through the air and amidst the long grass and from behind the cover of trees to our right we could make out Indians coming closer, some of them creeping on their bellies. Some of our men fell to their shot without ever making a move like tin soldiers at a midsummer fair and this gall'd us so our hands trembled and shook at our muskets with mixd fear and rage, the more when we heard the Savages whooping and yelling. Then we made out the grey uniforms of the French coming at us at a trot and yelling and singing that they supposd us turning tail at the sight of them. If God's truth be told we damn'd nearly did so for directly behind me, a fellow dropp'd his musket and crumpled on the ground and cried in a low way he was shot before he stoppd squirming and was at peace. And I heard others about me swear and pray and another set up a little moaning under his hat for we could now see them very plain two hundred yards no more, coming at us, some breaking into a run then dropping for cover and advancing again. It was an irregular jerky movement like tongues of fire darting hither and thither but all in our direction.

Still we held our pieces and the General himself he showed us his face and he was smiling an odd smile and holding his arm up and I could see his other hand had been shot away for there was blood on the sleeve of his fresh coat. And I could hardly bear to keep from going off for that flowing liquid feeling poured through my bowels and my heart banged inside my breast. No more than a hundred paces maybe and we could see their own faces now, their wigs all dirty and their run a kind of drunken stumble. Out of the corner of my eye I just saw Wolfe shout and drop his sword, the flash of it in the sun and the whole line barked out its volley; and we were sheltered in the great noise and smoke and smell of powder and dropd down to reload while the fellows at our backs let off their shot. We had done this so many times down below on the islands till it seemd a cloddish piece of obedience but now it servd us well as the volleys came so close together they made one great hellish thunder over and over again, echoing inside our heads and making our eyes swim and our throats choke. And when all that working and tamping and discharging were done and Mr Monckton ordered the cease, the silence seemed to come from a great hole we had torn in the body of their army. For as the light came through the smoke and the din faded, we could hear terrible screaming and saw the slaughter we had done and their backs running to the town. The

Highlanders began their shouting and with a skirl of pipes set after the French their broadswords out, but I was glad we didnt follow for I had little stomach for it.

Then up comes the Captain and tells me to take a message to the General to say our line had held and the enemy was put to flight. And I had rather it had be another man, I was tired at all we had done last night and this morning. But I obeyed and ran over the field stepping through blood and faces upturned in death and a few horses, poor beasts their bellies all spilld open. But the General was nowhere that the Brigadier had said, nor wherever I looked and I was making to go back down our line when I suddenly saw him, lying on a mound beside a sorry little bush attended by just two men, one leaning over and supporting Wolfe with his arm. Mr Browne for that was his name was begging him to lie and shouted at me to come fast and help. I approachd Wolfe and saw his face had gone stiff and greenish and his red hair glistened with sun and sweat. Blood had matted his belly where another ball had struck him and now more was oozing through his shirt and coat, so seeing he would not live I told him our news and in a groaning, gurgling sort of way I could hear him praise God for it.

In memory of John Clive, who knew all about the writing of history.

JULIAN BARNES

DRAGONS

LOUIS LE GRAND.

Anonymous contemporary print of Louis XIV depicted as *Le Roi Soleil*.

Pierre Chaigne, carpenter, widower, was making a lantern. Standing with his back to the door of his workshed, he eased the four oblongs of glass into the runners he had cut and greased with mutton fat. They moved smoothly and fitted well: the flame would be secure, and the lantern would cast its light in all directions, when this was required. But Pierre Chaigne, carpenter, widower, had also cut three pieces of beechwood the exact size of the panels of glass. When these were inserted, the flame would be cast in a single direction only, and the lantern would be invisible from three of the four compass points. Pierre Chaigne trimmed each piece of beechwood carefully, and when satisfied that they slid easily within the greased runners, he took them to a place of concealment among the discarded lumber at one end of the workshed.

Everything bad came from the north. Whatever else they believed, the whole town, both parts of it, knew that. It was the north wind, arching over the Montagne Noire, that made the ewes give birth to dead lambs; it was the north wind which put the devil into the widow Gibault and made her cry out, even at her age, for such things that she had to be stopped in the mouth with a cloth by her daughter, lest children or the priest hear what she wanted. It was to the north, in the forest on the other side of the Montagne Noire, that the Beast of Gruissan lived. Those who had seen it described a dog the size of a horse with the spots of a leopard, and many was the time, in the fields around Gruissan, that the Beast had taken livestock, even up to a small calf. Dogs sent by their masters to confront the Beast had had their heads bitten off. The town had petitioned the King, and the King sent his principal arquebusier. After much prayer and ceremony, this royal warrior had set off into the forest with a local woodsman, who shamefully had run away. The arquebusier emerged, several days later, empty-handed. He had returned to Paris, and the Beast had returned to its foraging. And now, they said, the dragons were coming, from the north, the north.

It was from the north, twenty years before, when Pierre Chaigne, carpenter, widower, had been a boy of thirteen, that the Commissioners had come. They had arrived, the two of them, lace at the wrist and severity upon the face, escorted by ten soldiers.

They had examined the temple and heard evidence, from those who came forward, concerning the enlargements that had taken place. The next day, from a mounting block, the senior of the Commissioners had explained the law. The King's Edict, he said, had given protection to their religion, that was true; but such protection had been awarded only to the religion as it had been constituted at the time of the Edict. There had been no licence to enlarge their cult: the enemies of the King's religion had been granted toleration but not encouragement. Therefore all churches built by the religion since the Edict were to be torn down, and even those churches which had merely been enlarged were to be torn down as warning and instruction to those who continued to defy the King's religion. Further, to purge their crime, it was the builders of the temple themselves who were to demolish it. Pierre Chaigne remembered at this point an outcry from those assembled. The Commissioner had thereupon announced that, in order to speed the work, four children from among the enemies of the King's religion had been placed under guard by the soldiers, and would be well and safely guarded, furnished with all that they required to eat, for as long as the dismantling of the temple might take. It was at this time that a great sadness came over the family of Pierre Chaigne, and shortly afterwards his mother had died of a winter fever.

And now the dragons were coming from the north. The priests of the King's religion had decreed that in the defence of the Holy Mother Church against the heretic anything was permissible, short of killing. The dragons themselves had another saying: What matter the road provided it lead to Paradise? They had come, not so many years before, to Bougouin de Chavagne, where they had cast several of the menfolk into a great ditch at the base of the castle tower. The victims, broken by their fall, lost as in the darkness of the tomb, had comforted themselves by singing the 138th Psalm. *'Though I walk in the midst of trouble, Thou wilt revive me: Thou shalt stretch forth Thine hand against the wrath of mine enemies, and Thy right hand shall save me.'* But as each night had passed, the voices from the great ditch had grown fewer, until the 138th Psalm was chanted no more.

The three soldiers placed into Pierre Chaigne's household were old men, forty years at least. Two of them had scars visible on their faces despite their great beards. On the shoulder of their leather tunics they wore the winged beast of their regiment. An additional whorl of stitching indicated to those with military knowledge that these old men belonged to the *dragons étrangers du roi*. Pierre Chaigne had no such understanding, but he had ears, and they were enough. These men did not seem to follow anything Pierre Chaigne said to them, and spoke among themselves the rough tongue of the north, the north.

They were accompanied by the secretary of the Intendant, who read a short decree to Pierre Chaigne and his assembled family. It being given that the household of Pierre Chaigne, carpenter, widower, by its wilful failure to pay the Tallage, was in odious breach of the King's law, the dragons, one officer and two men, would be quartered upon the Chaigne family, who were to supply such needs as they might have until such time as the household chose to pay the Tallage and raise the burden from themselves. When the secretary of the Intendant withdrew, one of the two common soldiers beckoned Pierre Chaigne's daughter Marthe towards him. As she advanced, he pulled from his pocket a small fighting animal which he held by the neck, and thrust it at her. Marthe, though merely thirteen years of age, had no fear of the beast; her calmness encouraged the family and surprised the soldier, who returned the creature to the long pocket stitched into the side of his trouser.

Pierre Chaigne had been accounted an enemy of the King's religion, and thereby an enemy of the King, but he did not admit to either condition. He was loyal to the King, and wished to live in peace with the King's religion; but this was not permitted. The Intendant knew that Pierre Chaigne could not pay the Tallage imposed, or that if he did pay it, the Tallage would immediately be increased. The soldiers had been placed into the household in order to collect the Tallage; but their very presence, and the cost of entertaining them, diminished still further any chance of payment. This was known and established.

The Chaigne household consisted of five souls: Anne Rouget, widow, sister of Pierre Chaigne's mother, who had come to them when her husband, a two-plough labourer, had died; after burying her husband according to the rites of the King's religion, she had accepted the cult of her sister's family. She had now passed fifty years of age, and was consequently growing feeble of mind, but still able to cook and make the house with her great-niece Marthe. Pierre Chaigne had also two sons, Henri, aged fifteen, and Daniel, aged nine. It was for Daniel that Pierre Chaigne felt the greatest alarm. The law governing the age of conversion had been twice changed. When Pierre himself had been an infant, it was established law that a child was not permitted to leave the church of his parents until he be fourteen years old, that age being considered sufficient to confirm mental capacity. Then the age had been reduced to twelve. But the new law had lowered it still further, to a mere seven years of age. The purpose of this change was clear. A child such as Daniel, not yet having that fixity of mind which comes with adult years, might be lured from the cult by the colours and scents, the finery and display, the fairground trickery of the King's religion. It was known to have happened.

The three *dragons étrangers du roi* indicated their needs with incomprehensible speech and lucid gesture. They were to occupy the bed, and the Chaigne family were to sleep where they liked. They were to eat at the table, the Chaigne family were to wait upon them and eat whatever they left. The key to the house was surrendered to the officer, as also were the knives which Pierre and his elder son naturally carried to cut their food.

The first evening, as the three soldiers sat waiting for their soup, the officer roared at Marthe as she was placing the bowls before them. His voice was loud and strange. 'My stomach will think that my throat is cut,' he shouted. The other soldiers laughed. Marthe did not understand. The officer banged on his bowl with his spoon. Then Marthe understood, and brought his food swiftly.

The secretary of the Intendant had stated that the dragons had lawfully been placed into the Chaigne household to collect the Tallage; and on the second day the three soldiers did make some attempt to discover any money or valuable property that might have been hidden. They turned out cupboards, looked beneath the bed, rooted in Pierre Chaigne's woodstacks. They searched with a kind of dutiful anger, not expecting to find anything concealed, but wishing it to be known that they had done what was formally demanded of them. Previous campaigns had taught them that the households they were first invited to occupy were never those of the rich. When their services had initially been engaged, many years ago at the end of the War, it had seemed obvious to the authorities to quarter the dragons with those who were best able to pay the Tallage. But this method proved slow; it strengthened the sense of fraternity among members of the cult, and produced some notable martyrs, the memory of whom often inspired the obstinate. Therefore it had been found more profitable to place the soldiers in the first instance into the families of the poor. This produced a useful division among the enemies of the King's religion, when the poor observed that the rich were exempt from the sufferings inflicted upon them. Swift conversions were many times thus obtained.

On the second evening, the soldier who kept the ferret in his long knee-pocket pulled Daniel on to his knee as the boy offered him some bread. He grasped Daniel so firmly by the waist that the infant immediately began to struggle. The soldier held in his free hand a knife with which he intended to cut his bread. He put the blade flat against the table, which was made from the hardest wood known to Pierre Chaigne, carpenter, widower, and with only a gentle push raised a crisp, transparent curl from the surface of the table.

''Twould shave a mouse asleep,' he said. Pierre Chaigne and his family did not understand these words; nor did they need to.

On the next day the soldiers used the ferret to slaughter a cockerel, which they ate for dinner, and finding the house cold at midday, though the sun was shining, they broke up two chairs and burnt them in the chimney, ignoring the pile of firewood beside it.

Unlike the King's religion, the cult could be celebrated anywhere that the faithful gathered, without attendance at the temple. The dragons made efforts to prevent the family of Pierre Chaigne from fulfilling their observances: the house was locked at night, and the three soldiers disposed themselves during the day so that they could spy upon the movements of the family. But they were outnumbered by five to three, and it happened sometimes that escape was possible, and thereby a visit to a house where the cult was being celebrated. Pierre Chaigne and his family openly talked of such matters in front of the dragons; and it seemed a kind of sweet revenge to do so. But the dragons in the town, who numbered around forty, had sources of intelligence, and although the members of the cult frequently changed the house in which they met, they were as frequently discovered by the soldiers. So the enemies of the King's religion chose to gather in the open air, in the forest to the north of the town. At first they met by day, and later only by night. Many feared that the Beast of Gruissan would descend upon them in the darkness, and the first prayer offered up was always a plea to be defended from the Beast. One night they were surprised by the dragons, who ran at them screaming, then beat and cut them with their swords, chasing them from the forest. The next morning, when the widow Gibault was not to be found, they returned to the forest and discovered her there, dead of the shock.

Pierre Chaigne was able to remember a time when the two populations of the town moved freely among one another, when a funeral or a marriage was celebrated by the whole community, without regard for the creed of the participants. It was true that neither the adherents of the King's religion nor the members of the cult would enter one another's place of ritual; but one group would wait patiently outside for the ceremony to be completed, and then the whole town would follow, whether to the graveyard or to the wedding feast. But shared rejoicing and shared grief had fallen equally into desuetude. Similarly, it was now rare in the town for a family to contain members of both faiths.

Though it was summer, the dragons were in need of fire. They burnt all the furniture except that which they needed for their own use. Then they began to burn the finest wood of Pierre Chaigne, carpenter, widower. Lengths of weathered oak from trees cut by his father twenty years ago, prime sections of elm and ash, all were consumed by fire. To increase Pierre Chaigne's indignity and misery, he was himself made to saw the timber into combustible lengths. When the dragons observed that this fine wood burnt more slowly than they had hoped, they ordered Pierre Chaigne and his sons to build a great bonfire beside the workshed, and instructed them to keep the fire alight until all Pierre Chaigne's wood was consumed.

As Pierre Chaigne stood looking at the mound of ashes which was all that remained of his future as a carpenter, the officer said to him, 'God's help is nearer than the door.' Pierre Chaigne did not understand these words.

Next the soldiers took all Pierre Chaigne's tools, and those of his son Henri, and sold them to members of the King's religion. At first Pierre Chaigne felt his misery lift, for having deprived him of his timber the soldiers did him no further harm depriving him of his tools; and besides, the sale of all his fine implements might even bring in money enough to pay the Tallage and so make the soldiers depart. However, the dragons sold Pierre Chaigne's tools not for their value, but for a price so low that no one could resist buying them, and then kept the money for themselves. François Danjon, miller, widower, member of the King's religion, who had bought several of the instruments, returned them to Pierre Chaigne under cover of darkness. Pierre Chaigne wrapped them in oiled cloths and buried them in the woods against a better day.

It was at this time that a pedlar, aged nineteen, passing through the town on foot from the direction of the Cherveux, was seized by several dragons and interrogated. He had the suspicious accent of the south. After being beaten, he admitted to membership of the cult; after being beaten further, he admitted that he desired to abjure. He was taken before the priest, who gave him absolution and copied his name into the register of abjuration. The pedlar made a mark beside his name, and two of the dragons, proud of their zeal and trusting that it would be recompensed, signed as witnesses. The pedlar was sent on his way without his goods. Henri Chaigne, aged fifteen, watched the beating, which was done in the public square; and as the victim was taken off to the church, a dragon whom he had not before seen said to him in the coarse language of the north, 'What matter the road provided it lead to Paradise?' Henri Chaigne did not understand what was being said, but recognized the word Paradise.

At first conversions came quickly, among the old, the feeble, the solitary, and those infants who had been forcibly beguiled by gaudy display. But after a few weeks the number of abjurations diminished. This was often the pattern, and it was known that the dragons frequently gave way to excesses in order that the conversions continue.

When the Tallage had first been announced, there were those who had sought to flee, who had heard that it was possible to reach St. Nazaire and discover the promised land elsewhere. Two families had left the town in this manner, whereupon members of the cult had been instructed by the Intendant to pull down and destroy with fire the houses they had left behind, whereupon the unpaid Tallage was not forgotten but transferred to those who remained. It was always this way. When a heretic converted to the King's religion, his Tallage was divided among the community of heretics, and their tax thus became even larger as their means of payment diminished. This led some to despair; but others, having lost everything, were made the more determined not to lose that faith on whose account they had already lost everything. Thus the booted missionaries met with more resistance as their work continued. This too was known and expected.

It was not long after Pierre Chaigne's instruments had been sold that Anne Rouget, his mother's sister, fell into sickness and became the first member of the family to abjure. When the dragons saw that she was weak and feverish, they yielded the bed to her and slept upon the floor. This chivalry was deliberate, for no sooner was she positioned in the bed than the soldiers declared her sickening unto death and summoned the priest of the King's religion. It was established by royal ordinance that when a Protestant heretic was dying, the priest had the right to visit the deathbed and offer the suffering one an opportunity to return in death to the Holy Mother Church. This visit, which the family were forbidden to prevent, was to take place in the presence of a magistrate; and the priest was not allowed to use any duress when attempting to obtain a conversion. However, such terms and conditions were not always strictly followed. The magistrate being occupied elsewhere, the priest was accompanied into the Chaigne household by the officer of the dragons. The family was expelled into the day's heat, two dragons guarded the door, and at the end of six hours Anne Rouget had been received back into the church where she had spent the first twenty years of her life. The priest departed with satisfaction, and that night the soldiers reclaimed the bed as their own and returned Anne Rouget to the floor.

'Why?' asked Pierre Chaigne.

'Leave me in peace,' replied Anne Rouget.

'Why?'

'One or the other is true.'

She did not speak beyond that, and died two days later, though whether from her fever, her despair or her apostasy Pierre Chaigne was unable to determine.

The child Daniel, aged nine, was the next to abjure. He was taken to the church of the King's religion, where it was explained to him that Anne Rouget, who had done the service of a mother for him, was awaiting him in Heaven, and that he would surely see her again one day unless he clung to heresy and chose to burn in Hell. Then he was shown fine vestments and the gilt reliquary containing the little finger of Saint Boniface; he smelt the incense and examined the monsters carved between the choir stalls— monsters which he would doubtless meet in person if he freely chose to burn in Hell. And the following Sunday, during the Mass, Daniel Chaigne publicly abjured the cult of the temple. His conversion was received with great and impressive solemnity, and afterwards he was much petted by the women of the King's religion. The following Sunday Pierre Chaigne and his elder son tried to prevent the dragons taking Daniel Chaigne to the Mass; they were beaten and the boy was taken none the less. He did not return, and Pierre Chaigne was informed by the priest that he had been placed beyond the reach of treason in the Jesuit college on the other side of the Montagne Noire, and that his education there would be at the expense of the family until such time as they chose to repudiate their heresy.

Only the obstinate ones now remained among the heretics. It was at this point that the Intendant named as Collector of the Tallage the leading Protestant landowner of the region, Pierre Allonneau, sieur de Beaulieu, fermier de Coutaud. It became his legal duty instantly to pay the accumulated tax owed by all members of the cult since the Tallage was announced. This he was unable to do, but being reduced at once to ruin, was no longer able to help in secrecy the obstinate ones.

The three dragons had been within the Chaigne household for two months. All the chickens and both the pigs had been eaten; all but a little of the furniture had been burnt; Pierre Chaigne's timber had been consumed with the exception of a rough pile of worthless lumber at the back of his shed. Others in the town who might have supported the family were now equally destitute. Each day Pierre Chaigne and his son Henri were obliged to traverse the woods and fields to obtain food. Two of the soldiers came with them, leaving the officer to guard Marthe. It was difficult to find enough food to satisfy six mouths, and the two dragons offered no assistance in the chase of a rabbit or the search for mushrooms. When there was not enough food for the soldiers to eat until they belched, the Chaigne family went hungry.

It was on their return from one of these daily expeditions that Pierre Chaigne and Henri Chaigne discovered that the officer had taken Marthe Chaigne, aged thirteen, into the bed with him. This sight caused Pierre Chaigne much anger and despair; only his religion prevented him from seeking that very same night the death of the officer.

The following day the officer chose to accompany the two heretics on the search for food, and one of the ordinary soldiers stayed behind to guard Marthe. This soldier also took her into the bed with him. No explanation was offered, and none was required. Marthe Chaigne refused to talk to her father or her brother about what had been done.

After nine days of seeing his sister taken as a whore, Henri Chaigne abjured his faith. But this action did not prevent the dragons from continuing to take his sister as a whore. Consequently, at the celebration of Mass the following Sunday, Henri Chaigne spat out of his mouth the holy wafer and the holy wine he had received from the priest. For this blasphemy against the body and blood of Our Lord, Henri Chaigne was duly tried by the bishop's court, condemned to death, and handed over to the soldiers who burnt him with fire.

Afterwards, the three soldiers separated Pierre Chaigne and his daughter, not permitting them to talk to one another. Marthe kept the house and whored for the dragons; her father hunted for nourishment and cut wood in the forest, since the autumn air was now turning cold. Pierre Chaigne, who had suffered greatly, was resolved to resist apostasy even unto death. His daughter was equally certain in her faith, and underwent her daily ordeal with the fortitude of a martyr.

One morning, after the officer had taken her into the bed with him but treated her less roughly for once, she received a brutal surprise. The officer had been accustomed to talk to her in the rough language of the north while he used her as a whore, to shout words and afterwards to mutter quietly. She had become familiar with this, and at times it helped her bear the suffering more easily, for she was able to imagine that the man who spoke these words from the north was himself as distant as the north.

Now, as he still lay athwart her, he said, 'You are brave, young girl.'

It took her a moment to realize that he had spoken her own language. He raised himself on an elbow and shunted himself off her. 'I admire that,' he went on, still in her language, 'and so I want to spare you further suffering.'

'You speak our tongue.'

'Yes.'

'So you have understood what we have said in the house since you came here?'

'Yes.'

'And the others too?'

'We have been in your country many years.'

Marthe Chaigne was silent. She remembered what her brother Henri had openly said about the dragons, and about the priest of the King's religion. Her father had revealed where the cult was to be celebrated, little suspecting the consequences. She herself had uttered words of hatred.

'And because I wish to spare you suffering,' the officer continued, 'I shall explain what will happen.'

What could happen? More pain of this kind. Worse. Torture. Death. No doubt. But then Paradise, surely.

'What will happen is that you will become with child. And then we shall testify that your father used you as a whore in our presence. And you will be taken before the court, your father and you, and there condemned. You will be burnt to death, you and your father, as also will be the child of this incestuous union within you.'

The soldier paused, and allowed the rigid girl fully to understand what he had said. 'You will abjure. You will abjure, and thereby you will save your father's life.'

'My father would rather die.'

'Your father does not have the choice. Only you have the choice whether your father dies or not. So you will abjure.'

Marthe Chaigne lay motionless in the bed. The soldier got up, adjusted his clothing roughly, and sat at the table waiting for her to agree. He was wise enough in his profession not to add unnecessary words.

Eventually the girl said, 'Where do you come from?'

The soldier laughed at the unexpectedness of the question. 'From the north.'

'Where? *Where?*'

'A country called Ireland.'

'Where is that?'

'Beyond the water. Near to England.'

'Where is that?'

'Beyond the water too. In the north.'

The girl in the bed remained with her head turned away from the soldier. 'And why do you come so far to persecute us?'

'You are heretics. Your heresy endangers the Holy Mother Church. All, everywhere, have a duty to defend Her.'

'Thirty pieces of silver.'

The officer appeared close to anger, but kept in mind the purpose of the day.

'If you have not heard of England then you have not heard of Cromwell.'

'Who is he?'

'He is dead now.'

'Is he your King? Did he recruit you? To come here and persecute us?'

'No. On the contrary.' The soldier began to remember things it did no good to remember, things which had fixed his life for ever, many years ago. Childhood, its sights, and its terrifying sounds. The harsh voices of England. 'Yes, I suppose he did. He recruited me, you could say.'

'Then I curse his name and all his family.'

The officer sighed. Where could he begin? There was so much to unravel, and he was an old man now, past forty. The child did not even know where England was. Where could he begin? 'Yes,' said the officer wearily. 'You curse his name. I curse his name too. We both curse his name. And on Sunday you will abjure.'

That Sunday, while incense stung her nostrils and her eye was assailed by the whorish colours of the King's religion, Marthe Chaigne, aged thirteen, her heart burdened by the sorrow she was causing her father and the knowledge that she would never be permitted to explain, abjured her faith. She made a mark on the register beside her name, and the officer of the dragons signed as witness. After he had signed, he looked up at the priest and said, in his own language, 'What matter the road provided it lead to Paradise?'

Marthe Chaigne was taken that day to the Union Chrétienne on the other side of the Montagne Noire, where she would be educated by the good sisters. The cost of her education would be added to the Tallage owed by Pierre Chaigne.

The following week the dragons left the town. The heretics had been reduced in number from 176 to eight. There were always the obstinate ones, but experience had shown that when they were greatly outnumbered they had little influence and ended their lives in bitterness and despair. The dragons were to move south and start their work in a new place.

The eight obstinate ones were burdened by the Tallage of those who had converted, with the cost of educating their own children as Catholics, and with numerous additional imposts. By ordinance they were forbidden from practising their trade or from hiring out their labour to members of the King's religion. They were also forbidden from abandoning their homes and seeking the promised land elsewhere.

Julian Barnes

Two nights after the dragons left, Pierre Chaigne, carpenter, widower, returned to his worked. He took down the lantern he had made and slid out three of its glass panels. From the pile of discarded lumber too contemptible even to be burnt by the soldiers he uncovered the three oblongs of thin beechwood. He pushed them gently between the runners sticky with mutton fat. Then he lit the candle and set the hood back in place. Lacking three-quarters of its glass, the instrument did not illuminate universally. But it gave a brighter, purer light for the direction in which it was pointed. Pierre Chaigne, carpenter, widower, would follow that light to the end of its journey. He walked to the door of his shed, lifted the latch, and set off into the cold night. The yellow beam of his lamp reached tremblingly towards the forest, where the other obstinate ones waited for him to join them in prayer.

RICHARD HOLMES
THE SAVAGE
NOTEBOOK

Sir Joshua Reynolds, *Portrait of Dr Samuel Johnson* (circa 1775).

Richard Savage remains a shadowy figure until the moment of his arrest for murder, in a back alley near Charing Cross, in November 1727. At that moment he steps into history: like a character walking out on to a brightly lit stage, into the glare of long-sought publicity. The public record of his life now begins: 'the man in black', as he is identified by a witness at the trial, is accused of killing James Sinclair in a brothel brawl at Robinson's Coffeehouse with a single, nine-inch sword-thrust, and wounding the maid Mary Rock on the head as she tried to prevent his escape. He enters history as a man on trial for his life; and the whole of his biography retains that element of *procès verbal*, a cross-questioning of identity, motive, character and extenuating circumstance, until seventeen years later it finds its most powerful advocate in the young Samuel Johnson whose superb, rhetorical speech for the defence forms the first, and perhaps the greatest, of the *Lives of the Poets*.

Up to that moment in 1727, when Savage was probably aged thirty, the definite facts of his life, as the sources for them, are minimal. Not even a portrait exists. The circumstances of his birth in Holborn are obscure; his claim to be the illegitimate and persecuted son of Lady Anne Macclesfield and the late Lord Rivers is doubtful. He was the author of two plays and of a handful of published poems. He had associated with the great journalist Richard Steele and worked anonymously for Alexander Pope collecting scurrilous material for *The Dunciad*. He was the subject of three articles in Aaron Hill's literary magazine *The Plain Dealer*, in 1724, characteristically pressing his claim for recognition and financial support from Lady Macclesfield. Here he had struck the first of his elegant, Romantic poses, drawing with something like genius on the established eighteenth-century archetype of the Distressed Poet—*der armer Poet*—celebrated by Hogarth and many others, already pressing his identity into new biographical form:

Hopeless, abandoned, aimless, and oppress'd
Lost to Delight, and every Way, distress'd;
Cross his cold Bed, in Wild Disorder thrown,

Thus sigh'd Alexis, *friendless, and alone—*
'Why do I breathe?—What Joy can Being give?
When she, who gave me Life, forgets I live!'

For Savage, 'she, who gave me Life,' is not the Muse as cruel lover. She is a more primitive, psychopathic obsession, and yet decorously Augustan: the Muse as cruel Mother, a rejection both sentimental and social. It was a phrase to which Johnson would respond with massive power and sympathy; and which Savage, with his brilliant and unaccountable perversity, would later tell Johnson he had never actually written.

The historical sources for Savage's trial and imprisonment are more extensive and detailed than for any other part of his career, except for the last months of his friendship with the young Johnson. They consist of an edited transcript of the court proceedings on 7 December, which lasted eight hours; this was subsequently published in 'Select Trials for Murder, Robberies, Rapes, Sodomy, Coining, Frauds and Other Offences at the Sessions-House in the Old Bailey, To which are Added, Genuine Accounts of the Lives, Behaviour, Confessions, and Dying Speeches, of the Most Eminent Convicts'; a set of manuscript *Notes* made of the cross-questioning of witnesses by Alexander Pope, who evidently attended the proceedings and later gave Savage five guineas towards prison expenses; a publicity pamphlet, organized by Aaron Hill within a few days of the conviction as part of a campaign to obtain a royal pardon, 'The Life of Mr Richard Savage . . . With some very remarkable Circumstances relating to the Birth and Education, of that Gentleman, which were never yet made publick'; some passing observations by Henry Fielding on Savage's deportment, including the suggestive detail that the poet, who habitually dressed in black, ordered a special suit of red velveteen to be executed in; finally there are Savage's own letters from Newgate prison and his reflections and dreams about the killing, which subsequently appeared in his major poem *The Wanderer*:

Now Sleep to Fancy parts with half his Power,
And broken Slumbers drag the restless Hour.

The Murder'd seems alive, and ghastly glares,
And in dire Dreams the conscious Murderer scares:
Shows the yet-spouting Wound, the ensanguined Floor,
The Walls yet-smoking with the spattered Gore . . .

From the transcript of the trial, it is indisputable that Savage and his two drinking friends, Gregory and Merchant, initiated the brawl at Robinson's at about two a.m., by threatening to strike the landlady with a chair, kicking over a table, and demanding that Sinclair and his companions 'deliver your Swords, god damn ye'. It is less clear what exactly occurred in the subsequent sword-fight—particularly who drew swords first—except that it was undoubtedly Savage who delivered the fatal thrust to Sinclair and wounded the maid Mary Rock. Savage himself never disputed these two facts.

His defence was surprisingly high-minded: first, that though he was not drunk, the whole episode was unpremeditated and an act of 'casual Passion'. Second, that his adversary and the witnesses against him were young, violent, disreputable persons of known 'low character', who gave contradictory evidence. Third, that he had been forced to defend himself against Sinclair, who was preparing to attack him, and that 'neither Reason nor Law obliged a Man to wait the Blow which was threatened, and which, if he should suffer it, he might never be able to return'. He explained his attack on Mary Rock in terms which Johnson recorded without comment: 'With regard to the Violence with which he endeavoured his escape, he declared, that it was not his Design to fly from Justice, or decline a Trial, but to avoid the Expenses and Severities of a Prison, and that he intended to have appeared at the Bar without compulsion.'

Savage took over an hour to argue these points in court. The most significant of them was clearly the plea of self-defence against Sinclair's threatened attack. Johnson makes much of this and of the bias of the witnesses against him. However, Johnson deliberately omitted from his magisterial account mention of a single but crucial piece of impartial forensic evidence, which was given by a medical surgeon who attended Sinclair as he was dying. This evidence emerged under cross-examination of the surgeon and is recorded in the transcript; Johnson must have read it. It shows as clearly as anything can in the confusion of a late-night brawl by candle-light, that from the very nature of Sinclair's wound and his stance when he received it he was not at that moment threatening Savage, or even facing him. The cross-questioning begins with the testimony of a nightwatchman called to the scene, and continues with that of the surgeon.

John Wilcox, another Watchman: 'I saw the Deceased leaning his Head upon his Hand, and then I heard the Deceased say: I am a Dead Man, and was stabbed cowardly.'

Mr Wilkey, the Surgeon: 'I searched the Wound, it was on the left Side of the Belly, as high as the Navel. The Sword had grazed on the Kidney, and I believe that Wound was the Cause of his Death.'

Court: 'Do you think the Deceased could receive that Wound in a posture of Defence?'

Mr Wilkey: 'I believe he could not, except he was Left-handed.' No evidence was ever produced to suggest that Sinclair was left-handed, and Johnson is silent on the entire exchange.

Instead, in his weighty summary of the trial, Johnson directs the reader's attention away from Savage's actual behaviour that night and the evidence regarding it. Instead, with great skill, he concentrates on circumstantial matters in order to gain sympathy for Savage and to suggest that he was somehow more of a victim than the murdered man.

> The Nature of the Act for which he had been tried was in itself doubtful; of the Evidences which appeared against him, the Character of the Man was not unexceptionable, that of the Women notoriously infamous; she whose Testimony chiefly influenced the Jury to condemn him, afterwards retracted her Assertions. He always himself denied that he was drunk, as had been generally reported. Mr *Gregory*, who is now Collector of *Antegua*, is said to declare him far less criminal than he was imagined, even by some who favoured him: And *Page* himself afterwards confessed, that he had treated him with uncommon Rigour. When all these Particulars are rated together, perhaps the Memory of *Savage* may not be much sullied by his Trial.

Johnson's remarks on Mary Rock, Gregory and Judge Page have
no other source than Savage's own reminiscences.

Savage's life and career show overwhelming instability in
personal relations, outbursts of anger and violence,
moodiness, grudge-bearing, endless financial sponging,
gloominess, suicidal tendencies, complete unreliability in
professional matters. Yet none of this is what his friends
remembered or valued. To them he was first of all a man of
extraordinary style and charm, gravely humorous, exquisitely
good-mannered, a born raconteur. He acted like a gentleman,
even ridiculously like a gentleman, though he was often so
poverty-stricken as to have no proper lodgings and no proper shoes.
His grandeur teetered on the borders of the absurd. Johnson's
friend Sir John Hawkins, himself a biographer, caught this in a
touching and ironic image: 'He was a handsome, well-made man,
and very courteous in the modes of salutation. I have been told, that
in taking off his hat and disposing it under his arm, and in his bow,
he displayed as much grace as those actions were capable of; and
that he understood the exercise of a gentleman's weapon, may be
inferred from the use he made of it in that rash encounter . . . '

Savage's deportment during the trial, and later in Newgate while
under sentence of death, gives us some of our earliest and most vital
glimpses into his complex, brilliant and possibly pathological
character. One episode during the trial is especially revealing. The
Judge, Justice Page, was well-known not only for his severity, but
for acute and often damaging witticisms at the expense of
defendants he did not like. He was later lampooned by both Pope
and Fielding for this. In his summing-up, he turned the jury's
sympathy against Savage (though they may not have needed much
turning) by cleverly mocking Savage's gentlemanly airs. In doing
so, he deliberately touched on Savage's most vulnerable aspect, his
obsession with illegitimate birth and supposed nobility as the son of
Lady Macclesfield.

> Gentleman of the Jury, you are to consider, that Mr
> Savage is a very great man, a much greater man than you
> or I, Gentleman of the Jury; that he wears very fine

clothes, much finer clothes than you or I, Gentleman of the Jury; that he has abundance of money in his pocket, much more Money than you or I, Gentleman of the Jury; but, Gentleman of the Jury, is it not a very hard Case, Gentleman of the Jury, that Mr Savage should therefore *kill* you or me, Gentleman of the Jury?

Savage was so incensed by this mockery that he interrupted Judge Page and, according to Johnson, 'resolutely asserted that his Cause was not candidly explained.' Twice ordered to be silent, he continued to interrupt the judge and was finally dragged from the bar by force. This display of temper no doubt damaged his case with the jury quite as much as the evidence of hostile witnesses. But here Johnson's observation is both acute and candid. For this part of Judge Page's summary exists nowhere in the court transcript. Instead, Johnson gives it 'as Mr Savage used to relate it', many times afterwards to his friends, acting out the 'eloquent Harangue' with ironic amusement at his own position. Suddenly one begins to see why Johnson admired his indomitable spirit and courage in the face of personal disaster.

When the guilty verdict was delivered, Merchant was convicted of manslaughter (he had not been armed) and was branded in the hand; Savage and Gregory were condemned to public hanging at Tyburn. Savage's prison conditions deteriorated after sentencing: he was put in close confinement at Newgate—previously he had the relative freedom of the Press Yard—and his legs were loaded with fifty-pound iron weights.

His inner state is reflected in many passages of *The Wanderer*: how 'the Dungeon-glooms hang heavy on his Mind', how he falls asleep and dreams of liberty, until with a sudden crash of bars, 'he starts, wakes, storms, and all is Hell within'. He imagines his coming execution in the person of various half-fictional figures. His confessional verse occasionally strikes a new note, a personal intensity quite alien to the decorous world of Pope and Thomson. It has a high, keening spiritual anguish, a sense of personal disintegration and loss, which once more prefigures Romanticism, and which the young Johnson was the first to value and appreciate.

Cosmo, as Death draws nigh, no more conceals
That Storm of Passions, which his Nature feels;
He feels much Fear, more Anger, and most Pride;
But Pride and Anger make all Fear subside.
Dauntless he meets at length untimely Fate;
A desperate Spirit! rather Fierce, than Great.
Darkling he glides along the dreary Coast,
A sullen wandering, self-tormenting Ghost.

The vision of that last couplet, with its unappeased unending landscape of loss and exile, is as terrible as any Classical underworld or Christian Purgatory. It is a glimpse of the drowned world of Cowper's *Castaway* and Coleridge's *Mariner*.

But however self-tormented, desperate or guilty, Savage did not give way. He seems to have been sustained by the very extremity of his situation and by the glamour and publicity it brought him. To his many visitors in prison, he played out his new role as the gentleman-poet at bay. It is clear that for the first time in his life he had achieved a measure of the recognition he sought. To his supposed mother, Lady Macclesfield, he sent dignified appeals for help. (Johnson records how these were rejected, and in one of his fiercest passages speculates that she actually pressed for his execution, by putting about at court lurid tales of Savage once threatening to murder *her*. 'Thus had Savage perished by the Evidence of a Bawd, a Strumpet, and his Mother . . . ' There were more to the tales than Johnson cared to admit.)

Determined that his story should never be forgotten, Savage secretly collaborated (as he afterwards half-acknowledged) with the author of the publicity pamphlet, vividly describing not only his trial but the many misfortunes of his early life. He took great care that his final speech at the bar, with its fine nonchalant flourishes, should be carefully transcribed. He already saw the justification for his wayward, indigent, persecuted life (as he saw it) in terms of his biography as well as his poetry. He wished to appeal to a higher, historical court. Indeed it was to be this document, which anticipates the popular conventions of the *Newgate Calendar*, and its lives of 'eminent convicts', that Johnson would eventually transform into the first great essay in modern literary biography. Pleading the cause of a convicted criminal, with all the power, subterfuge and humanity at his command, Johnson would establish a higher justice, a new genre of trial.

Why Johnson should have chosen to defend Savage, and how an intimate friendship between two such apparently opposing characters could ever have formed, is a singular mystery. Sir John Hawkins called it 'the one particular Event' in Johnson's career that seemed hardest to explain. Mrs Thrale simply thought he was misled by 'the goodness of his Heart'. While Boswell grew positively indignant over the whole matter, describing Savage as 'a man, of whom it is difficult to speak impartially, without wondering that he was for some time the intimate companion of Johnson; for his character was marked by profligacy, insolence and ingratitude . . . ' But these judgements come from friends (and biographers) of the later Johnson. None of them knew personally of the young Johnson, the restless, unhappy, poverty-stricken writer who ranged the backstreets of the city by night and day.

Johnson's choice of Savage as friend, and as biographical subject to be defended sometimes in the teeth of historical evidence, reveals a figure very different from the Great Augustan Moralist and Lexicographer. It reveals a Johnson who valued genius in an almost Romantic way. In his biography of Savage he would set character against deeds, creative vitality against social destruction, poetry against worldly success. Drawing on his own profound and lifelong sympathy with the outcast and oppressed, he would look at Augustan society in a new light and change our notion of what is important in human history. He would make the very individuality of a life its own plea. As he put it in the memorable, closing words of the *Life*: 'Those are no proper Judges of his Conduct who have slumbered away their Time on the Down of Plenty, nor will a Wise man easily presume to say, "Had I been in Savage's Condition, I should have lived, or written, better than Savage."'

Not that Richard Savage, 'son of the late Lord Rivers', would ever have admitted that a distressed poet and nobleman would deliberately stoop to such a vulgar appeal. He maintained his glamorous public pose until the royal pardon miraculously arrived on 6 January 1728. While still grimly preparing for Tyburn, he wrote jauntily to his friend Cibber with no mention of his nightmares, except to say that he had been plagued by the 'poor illiterate' Newgate padre asking for his confession. He added: 'The weight of my Fetters has so weakened me (being obliged to lie in them) that I can scarce drag myself across a room.—I could not help smiling this afternoon—a kind of Bookseller visited me, in order to solicit me for an Account of myself, to be printed at my decease.—What indecensies will not Wretches commit thro hopes of Money?'

© Richard Holmes

HISTORY

IN

GRANTA

To coincide with the publication of the *History* issue, Granta is offering the following issues of historical interest at the special price of £5:

Granta 12: Stanley Booth, *The True Adventures of the Rolling Stones.*

Stanley Booth's The True Adventures of the Rolling Stones is only in part about the musicians it depicts. It is also a social history and a confession—a chronicle in the tradition of Michael Herr's *Dispatches*, of people committed to their own destruction.

Granta 14: Autobiography.

'An outstanding collection.' *The Times.*

*Granta*17: Graham Greene, *While Waiting for a War.*

'I find myself in 1985 refreshing my memory of 1937 and 1938 in an old commonplace book and a very fragmented diary. There are verses copied there that I must have chosen for their significance at moments of my life; literary gossip, bizarre crimes and divorces wrenched from newspapers . . . and then suddenly the digging of trenches on Clapham Common.'

Each issue is available at £5 each. This offer expires on 31 August 1990. Send the coupon below (or details written on a separate sheet of paper) to Granta, 2/3 Hanover Yard, Noel Road, Islington, London N1 8BE.

Please send me the following back issues:

    Granta 12: Stanley Booth, *The True Adventures of the Rolling Stones.*

    Granta 14: Autobiography.

    Granta 17: Graham Greene, *While Waiting For a War.*

Name _____

_____

_____ Postcode _____

Payment: ☐ cheque enclosed

        ☐ credit card (subscriptions only) Access/American Express/
          Diners Club no._____ (Visa not accepted)

Credit card orders can be accepted by phone: (071) 704 0470
For foreign orders, add £1 for postage for each issue.

JINDRICH STREIT
SOVINEC IN MORAVIA

Jindrich Streit

B efore the Second World War there were sixty families—
most of them Sudeten Germans—and fifty-eight houses in
Sovinec, a small village in Czechoslovakia north-east of
Brno. Now there are only twenty-six people living in the eight
remaining habitable houses.

Jindrich Streit has lived here since he was ten. He cherished the
idea of chronicling the dying village and researched letters and
books, collected all the memories and material he could on the
history of Sovinec. 'Then,' he says, 'one day in 1975, I realized I
knew everything about the villagers except their faces.' And so he
began to photograph them. Patiently. One by one, as they went
about their everyday tasks. Later he walked to the neighbouring
village of Krisov and photographed its fifty inhabitants surrounded
by ruins and ghosts.

Streit was a school-teacher, like his father, but his photographs
proved too much for the Czech authorities, who in 1982 sacked him,
as they had done his father, and sent him to prison. On his release
Streit became a farm worker but continued his photography. He
also set about transforming his house, which had served as the
village school, into an art gallery where sculptures and traditional
paintings are now shown alongside those of Czech avant-garde
painters, who bring their work to be shown in Streit's large space
with its cold parquet floor.

This text is based on an article which appeared in *Libération*.

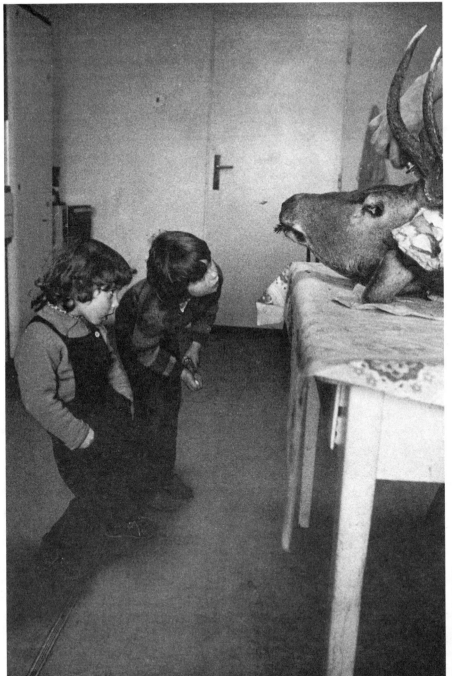

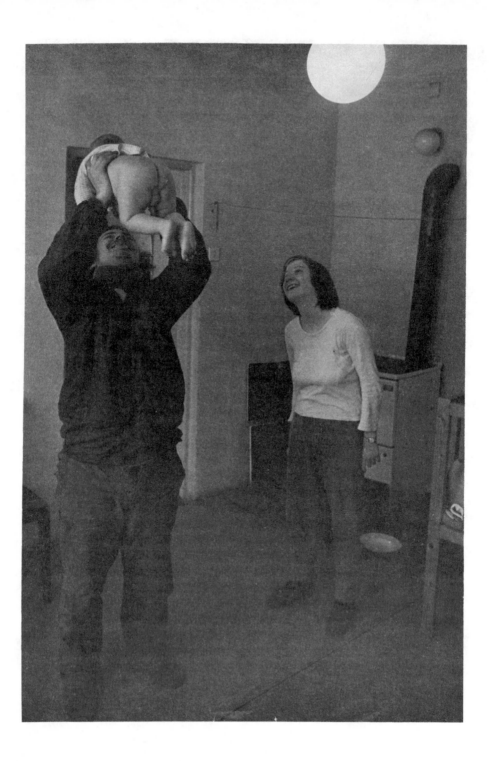

THE WHITE CUTTER

BY DAVID POWNALL

is the Confession of Hedric, who becomes the greatest architect of the thirteenth century. It tells of his unique education, of rogue clerics, singular nuns and The Four, a secret cabal teetering on the brink of genius and dementia. It reveals much about light and stone, God and the Devil, fathers and sons, the Church and the State, love and murder, our need for secrecy and for uncontradicted truth in an age of chaos.

'A superb piece of invention ... Britain's answer to *The Name of The Rose*'   *Listener*

'A cracking good tale, Pownall has touched before on the dark and arcane but never to such effect. He was always a good novelist. Now he is a major one' *Independent*

ELIZABETH HARDWICK
NEW YORK CITY:
CRASH COURSE

The old New York airport was once called Idlewild, a pastoral welcome to the gate of a zoological garden of free-ranging species. Or so it seemed to say before the names were changed to those of politicians, those who won. Kennedy Airport, international arrival to our hysterical, battered and battering, pot-holed, bankrupt metropolis. A spectacular warehouse this city is; folk from anywhere, especially from those sunny sovereignties to the south of us, coming to peer out of blackened windows, each one in his shelter of sorts.

In 1879 a curious urban structure called the 'dumb-bell tenement' won a prize as the most imaginative and useful design for the hordes seeking shelter. Windows looked out upon a rubbish-strewn courtyard, black and empty, giving neither light nor air but surely an improvement on something not previously thought of. Shelter, beautiful word, like dwelling. 'Wuthering Heights is the name of Mr Heathcliff's dwelling.' But utter not the word shelter just now, here where it has acquired or grown a scrofulous hide.

Will you not come with me to the Shelter on this icy evening, dear, old homeless one, stuffed into your bag of rags and surrounded by up-standing pieces of cardboard, making as it were a sort of private room on the freeze of concrete near a corner or before a store front? No, you f---ing little, rat-faced volunteer on vacation from the country club of Wellesley College or piling up credit at the Fordham School of Social Work. I'll die before I'll take my bag upon bag of nameless litter, my mangy head, my own, my leprous legs, purple, scabbed and swollen, my numbed, crooked fingers, myself, to the City Shelter, or flop house, whatever you call it.

It's a battle and the blue and white salvation van makes off slowly, idly offering in the gloom of perplexity the wide, public, rectangular barns, the dormitories with their rows of iron beds, muslin sheets and flattened pillow, and somewhere down a corridor a luke-warm shower. The trouble is, among others, that if you nod off, what you're there for, you might become separated from your wealth of trash, robbed of your cache of mementoes—an old key, a newspaper item perhaps of some paranoid interest, a safety-pin, an arcane Welfare Department communication without name or number—things folded into layers of astounding clothing; and worst of all to be with others.

The 1990 census is trying to take note of them, on the streets, in the tunnels of the subways, hiding behind a bush in the park, or on the lonesome late nights of the Westside Highway in the traffic dividing centre, standing by a metal can burning trash for warmth . . . Well, there's no news in that, not here in New York . . . When you get right down to it, the van driver said, the homeless people are just a bunch of clichés. Are they ever, said the volunteer girl.

In our antiquity, not so many hundred years ago, this place was lying here, entrance to the dreaming acres north, south and west, lying here waiting for something to happen for what's new? Waiting for the worn-down explorers trying to get to the orient, waiting for them to alight from their obdurate, temperamental ships, waiting for a sort of opening night in Manhattan. At last they paddled ashore to our Bay and didn't find much, indeed 'no indigenous civilization', or so they said. Not much except the usual basking verdure, several dozen or so small wind-rattled shelters made of tree bark and 'the poor Indian'. (Columbus, around Santa Domingo or thereabout, took several of these solemn, long-faced, reddish-brown bodies back to Europe for the curiosity of it and perhaps to amuse his wife, 'the well-born Dona Felipa Perestrello e Monia'; and as a sort of wampum offering the transported native stock was to receive Christian baptism, to implant in innocent minds the Happy Hunting Ground complexities of the Resurrection.)

It was to be New Amsterdam with the Dutch putting up lots for sale and beginning to imagine our fate-laden checker-board destiny. They bought, in a manner of speaking, the place and strangely the straggling settlers from the Zuider Zee, or IJsselmeer, initiated by a squatter's rights over the succeeding English, our aristocracy, 'old new York', born in the memory perhaps of the murdered William the Silent. Van Renssalaer, Schuyler and Schermerhorn, names with a somewhat heraldic resonance, supplanted the Ocnida and the Algonquin. And were themselves supplanted in the porous atmosphere of New York which will, by a vivacious regicide, crown more kings and queens in a year than history knows of.

A grey Sunday afternoon, smoky light, and a sanctified drowsing between our rivers East and West, a quiet except for the sacrificial athleticism of the joggers, running or preparing to run in the park, as a rabbit out of its hutch will surely hop off. And some comfortable cows still lolling in their stalls on Central Park West. All of this before the tiny white lights come on, a cheerful, if unnatural, decoration strung on the winter tree branches. Cottony brilliant leaves they are as the grinding bus, with a few Sunday evening travellers, makes its way through the underpass in the soft, waxy beauty of the urban evening.

At the Lincoln Center Opera House, papier mâché stone battlements by the ineffable Zefferelli, worth, or cost, a couple of million, a piece of the rock. Baudelaire said that what he liked best about the opera was the *chandelier* and here some invisible hand lowers the large bunch of little globes and raises them before dimming in a pretty display of mechanical superfluity. In 1849, at the Astor Place Opera House, there was a ferocious outbreak of riot, one of peculiar import. On the heath, thunder and lightning, torches and baseball bats 'hover through the fog and filthy air'. The occasion was a performance of Shakespeare's *Macbeth,* in the theatre which was then a shrine for the patroons who would trip in satin slippers through the horse-droppings at the curb, having emerged from the carriage to leave the coachman in chimney-sweep black outfittings to rust in the long wait for the final curtain. And then it would be off to the houses, the mansions, edging ever upward from the thirties streets near Madison to the fifties on Fifth Avenue, the way things were going. In the old postcards of the city everything appears gay, small, empty and tranquil. The swish of long skirts and the gothic ascension of many wonderful hats, worthy people treading the streets, down Broadway, and keeping away from the Plug-Uglies, the Dead Rabbits, citizen gangs with their own rancorous claims.

For the *Macbeth* performance the Anglophiles had brought across the Atlantic a star, William Macready, an innocent elocutionist, on tour. This was seen as an insult to our own master of fustian, Edwin Forrest, and the mob mounted a patriotic stone-throwing, window-smashing, outraged, red-faced, beer-encouraged assault. Poor Macready, eloquence trembling through the dagger irresolution and the pacing melancholy of tomorrow and tomorrow, and at last having surrendered his head to Macduff, was to slink through the back door with a cortège, front and back, of high prestige, among them Washington Irving and John Jacob Astor. Still, the contract was in place and at a later performance thousands gathered to storm the building, stones flying like some hellish hail-storm of local resentment. The rioters were met with 300 policemen and 200 state militia who fired into the crowd, killing almost two dozen of the rebels. Macbeth Macready decamped on the next boat to England but the theatrical criticism of the populace, the class gap, the canals of separation, already impassable, represented by the rioters and the merchant class, represented by the point-blank fire, occasioned the usual bitter civic debate, howls ending in a draw.

Herman Melville, home from the cannibals and acquainted with mutiny, getting on fairly well with *Omoo* and *Typee*, signed like a good PEN member the first petition favouring the appearance of Macready on the boards. This was before the militia assault and what he might have thought about the state's forceful, explosive protection of the right to speechifying is not certain. Melville's mother was a Ganesvoort, an 'old New Yorker'.

The emergency ambulance shrills through the night—or is it a fire truck, all glistening red and burnished brass shining in the murk, arriving in multiplication like a tank parade, the men in their black and yellow rubber mantles and their smart, brim-back hats, pirate hats, answering with good fortune this time only a waste-basket conflagration in the banal, sleepless interiors of ABC-TV. As early as seven in the morning, in the winds of winter or the breathless air of summer, the crowds gather outside the building to see great Pompey pass the streets of Rome, that is to see whoever might be interviewed on the morning show.

In 1838, on an arctic evening with temperatures sliding down to seventeen below zero, as if in the brush-strewn fields of Minnesota under a high, cold moon, there was a four-alarm flaming that swept through the stone and timber of the financial district. Thirteen acres turned to frozen rubble. They were soon back on the trading floor, as they are ever to be, mysterious men, *condotierri*, nowadays tanned from battle in the financing trenches, trim from the rigours of the conference call, nervous and powerful on their steeds, lances drawn, rulers of principalities in the Hamptons or in Beverly Hills. Should they be thrown from their horses they will be bathed in unguents, the precious oils of severance pay and bankruptcy bonuses, settlements. 'Day after day the columns of the press revealed fresh scandals to the astonished public, which at last grew indifferent to such revelations. Beneath all the wrangling of the courts, however, while the popular attention was distracted by the clatter of lawyer's tongues, the leaders in the controversy were quietly approaching a settlement.' (Charles Francis Adams on the Erie Railroad scandals of 1868.) A golden age it has been the last few years and about some of the financiers, soon to be tried and those tried before, you might say they wrote the script and played all the parts.

The men make and the wives spend, indeed are chosen for their talents in consumption, a contract historical, imitative and pleasurable as the sunshine. But, think what an occupation it is to fill the cathedrals, the vaults and domes on Park Avenue and Fifth. Ten coats of paint on the glaze of the walls and even then, so often, not quite right. A burdensome eclecticism of track lighting and electrified ceiling ornamentations transported from the castles of Europe. In an entrance hall, four or five eighteenth-century Dutch interiors; up higher on the avenue the collector is, as we say, 'into' contemporary and thus a Jasper Johns, bought yesterday, hangs over a leather sofa. Everywhere, gregarious tables to hold quaint miniatures, inlaid boxes, Georgian silver items; grand carpets from Xanadu, chairs from France, desks from England and in the dining hall, large enough for the knights in a saga, rare, fragile practicalities in lots of twenty-four for receiving food and drink. Unassuaged longings and who would imagine there was so much provenance left or waiting to be sold or traded. 'Stone by stone we shall remove the Alhambra, the Kremlin and the Louvre and build them anew on the banks of the Hudson.' (Benjamin de Casseres, *Mirrors of New York*.) A billion dollars is buying, arranging, dusting and polishing and insuring.

As for a mere million or two: Nothing much came forth from the red lips, the lithe, stalky, skin and bone woman in a mink tent getting out of the long, black, hired car. She emerges from the tomb and from the defiant optics of the black limousine windows, opaque as death on the outside, but from which she, inside, can look out to see a white poodle on its leash. I wish I had one, she says, and he, from the hearse in which they are driven, says, If you want one, buy one, for God's sake.

The black tube waits at the curb while they enter and loll for an hour or so, as if in a sudden resurrection, among the tropical plants of the lead-paned restaurant. The little French lamps on the table reveal luscious cakes waiting for the knife. But not for them. Perhaps for the two plump wage-earners from the 'boroughs', maliciously defining address, perhaps for them the infantile fatality of the gorgeous concoctions, all cream and gurgle and clog, life-threatening and shaming. The tomb-dwellers look on from their de-caf espressos.

The delivery boy from the Food Emporium is at the door. Theatrical youth, delivery youth, scarcely a boy. High-top running shoes with the laces slack, in the fashion, hair, also in the fashion, shaved from the nape of the neck to end in a pile at the top of the head beaming straight up as if struck by a thunderbolt— some name-brand mousse or spray helping to defy gravity. Around the streets they go, pushing their archival load: low-sodium seltzer water, Kosher hot dogs, low-cholesterol mayo, Perdue chicken breasts, Weight-Watchers margarine, four grain bread, Ben and Jerry's Chocolate Cherry Ice Cream, Paul Newman's marinara sauce . . . What the deliverer gets from the $2.50 charge for service is a corporate secret, but here he is, deer-fleet, smelling briskly of cologne, on the job.

Slavery came to the Manhattan shores with great promptitude, came to New Amsterdam with black souls gathered up by the prudent Dutch at Curaçao, another of the country's far-flung 'interests'. And more were to arrive later, after Amsterdam gave way to New York. A pitiful insurrection among the slaves of the city took place in 1712, a dream-heavy insufficiency of Black Power it was. A few dozen from Africa, with a musket here and there, went on a rampage, set a few fires, killed a few whites. You see the insurrectionists glistening and trembling, large, agonized, bewildered figures like the Emperor Jones, trying to run for cover up a tree, in a swamp, and soon overcome by the city militia. And taught a lesson, yes, strung up for public viewing, burned, tortured on the wheel. Consequent fear on the streets, in the houses, no place is safe, muggers (derivation unknown) on every corner, too many of them . . . and so on and so on.

There appeared in the fearful city a most extraordinary white lunatic, one Mary Burton, indentured, that is, a citizen from the British Isles working to pay off the cost of the passage to the New World, pay on the credit card more or less, many of them of course declining in clever ways after reaching their destination, here. When fires and robberies broke out, Mary B. began to offer her inside dope gained in taverns, her dense knowledge of bar-room alliances for felony. She took her interesting, fevered tales to the courts and thus set the slave-holders on edge for protection and revenge. Slaves hanged, burned at the stake, sent off somewhere, until Mary, wonderfully alert to the great industry of New York, alert to publicity, the magic of it, went astray, far afield, accusing respectable whites, whoever, and at last that was that for Mary. Slavery abolished in New York in 1799, too risky, not worth the bother, bottom-line.

City of journalism, the lone suitable literary art to catch up, take in this treasure island, open-faced, each street a logo, Fifth Avenue or Tenth Avenue, Duke Ellington Boulevard or Gramercy Park, Eastside and Westside, the Village, a transparency, laid out, as easy to read as an advertisement, nothing hidden. You know where you are and who will be there with you, a sort of suburbanism in the air. Someone must be doing the work, coming in of a morning, double-parking, arriving over the bridges and expressways to fix the leaking pipe, to paint the high-gloss walls, lay the Italian tiles, scrape the floors in a gas mask, deliver the heating oil flowing in the long, fat coils. They run the elevators, stand importantly in their tuxedos in the old-fashioned restaurants and at midnight take the subway train back to Brooklyn or Queens or Flushing or some other stop.

Nothing here in the brilliant inner city for the family man, place of torture and bankruptcy for the guards of the flaking, tedious columns of the Temple of Dendur at the Metropolitan Museum, for the news dealers, the movie ushers, the night workers with their pails and Dustbusters neatening at Rockefeller Center. The old shops in the West Thirties and on Seventh Avenue with their filthy windows announcing Wholesale—dusty ribbons for unwanted hats, plastic flowers, buttons and buttonholes, bolts of figured cotton for the homemade house dress, thread for the Singer Sewing Machine, guitar strings: establishments sitting on prime real estate, a joke, you might say, of mal-adaptation and swept away in a quick fluid movement, as if by the hose from the Sanitation truck.

The Italo-Americans on the street where the deputed mobster lives in a small bungalow with a Mercedes equal in size out front and little sign here of melting in the pot. The Salvadorans, the Dominicans, the Koreans in their fruit stores, the Asian Indians at the newspaper kiosk, hot dog vendors from Greece, huddling together somewhere, each one a secret, inviolable clan, getting by, offering product but, off the income bracket, unAmericanized, still breathing in the hills of home.

The Irish and many of the German immigrants to the city were not attracted to fighting for the Union and in honour of the Emancipation Proclamation. So, when the Conscription Act was passed in 1863, falling largely on the working classes and the unemployed whites without the money to buy off, the great Draft Riots broke out. The Irish, objects of contempt in New York and Boston, did not always share the Yankee high-minded grief for the stain of slavery on the national psyche. The Rainbow Coalition of Protestant, well-to-do abolitionists and the black population was the same it is now at the reign of our first black mayor. A horror of class and race war fell on the streets of Manhattan in 1863 as the rioters attacked the police, set fire to the Colored Orphan Asylum, lynched, broke into white abolitionist homes, set upon Horace Greeley's left-wing paper, the *Tribune*, and sent him flying out the back door or hiding under a table in fear of his life. 'It was the women who inflicted the most fiendish tortures upon Negroes, soldiers and policemen captured by the mob, slicing their flesh with butcher knives, ripping out eyes and tongues, and applying the

torch after victims had been sprayed with oil and hanged on a tree.'
(*The Gangs of New York*, by Herbert Asbury.)

The explorers seldom came to a good end. Columbus died in
want, ignorant of the fame that would attach his name to New
York City banks, avenues, universities, restaurants, dry-
cleaning establishments, video centres, delis—and many more. Sir
Walter Raleigh, after smoking tobacco and eating the corn of the
New World in Virginia, got into trouble with the Spanish and was
beheaded in London. 'What a head fell there,' said the executioner.
Verrazano was killed by the natives in the West Indies. Henry
Hudson and his son, after a leveraged buyout of the Hudson Bay
Company, were cast adrift to die up near Labrador, never to see the
Palisades again.

The truest New Yorker among the great seamen was Captain
Kidd, who, in his span of years kept going and coming here, married
a respectable and prosperous widow, Sarah Oort, and had a
daughter, built himself a brick house and gathered up other
properties. In the colonial period, Captain Kidd could be said to
know everyone worth knowing; he knew the legislator Robert
Livingston and the colonial governor of New England, Lord
Bellamont, both of whom were mixed up in his affairs and maritime
assignments and both abandoned him. Captain Kidd, sent out to
hunt pirates, was accused of turning pirate himself and of murdering
a troublesome seaman during a quarrel. The captain left some
treasure from the legal looting of captured ships at Gardiner's
Island on Long Island and left in romantic minds the possibilities of
hidden treasure elsewhere. Like our own, finally sentenced to death
or long imprisonment, he has had his defenders, investigative
reporters telling a different story. As for him, his defence is familiar
to New York ears, 'I am the innocentest person of them all, only I
have been sworn against by perjured persons.'

The noble mariners of old, taking off without a space suit and
nobody back in Europe on Mission Control, endured great
suffering and often with little profit to themselves. But, of course,
they would discover this America and the other America, South.
And yet imagine the United States at last, each state with its
boundaries and climate, mountains or flatlands for wheat; imagine

all the states with their borders and squawking pride without the immense, obstinate, unassimilable, violently fluent New York City. Imagine the sulky provinciality of a vast country freed from this 'unAmerican' city with its intimidating statistics of bodies, crimes, dope, guns, homicide records, robberies, illiterates, poverty, its blank towers, mausoleums hanging over the edge of the two rivers and blighting the rigid intersections in between, and its turbulent campaigns of consumption in the imperial mode.

From where have you come and why are you here? Why does the humming-bird return to the north? A puzzle, each resident of the recalcitrant city a puzzle. Once here a lingering infection seems to set in and the streets are filled with the complaints and whines of the hypochondriac who will not budge, will not face a fertile pasture. Here it is, that's all, the place itself, shadowy, ever promising and ever withholding, a bad mother, queen of the double-bind . . . Nevertheless.

> *Keep your fields of clover and timothy, and your cornfields and orchards,*
> *Keep the blossoming buckwheat fields where the Ninth-month bees hum;*
> *Give me faces and streets—give me these phantoms incessant and endless along the trottoirs!*
>
> Whitman

The constellations are not visible in the evening sky because of our impressive interference. Perhaps there, suddenly, is the red star, Denab, United Airlines coming into port, edging down so gracefully with its rosy flickering lights, an everlasting beacon in the over-loaded sky, saying, *prepare for landing.*

JONATHAN SPENCE
THE PARIS YEARS
OF ARCADIO HUANG

The Mansell Collection

Antoine Watteau (1684–1721), Drawing of a Chinese man.

Life was hard for Arcadio Huang in the autumn and early winter of 1713. Paris was bitterly cold and covered in fog. France's long war over the Spanish Succession had demoralized the population, driven up the cost of food and eroded the value of money. Arcadio had married a young Parisian woman, Marie-Claude Regnier, in April 1713; their life quickly became a struggle for survival and self-respect. Their rented room in rue Guénégaud, on the south bank of the Seine across from Notre Dame cathedral, was always cold since they had not enough money for a regular supply of wood or coal. Their furniture was sparse, they had few clothes and they could not afford a decent matrimonial bed. Salt for their simple meals was too expensive. And, worst of all, on some mornings Huang would awaken spitting blood. After these episodes he felt a terrible lassitude and would need to rest in bed for hours.

Huang was born in 1679 in the coastal Chinese province of Fujian. His father was a Catholic convert, baptized as Paul; anxious to live the celibate life of a religious Christian, Paul had wished not to marry, but had been forced to by his parents, since he was their only son and they would not allow the family line to die out. Paul's wife bore four daughters and the family was in despair. Then she gave birth to a boy, baptized as Arcadio. Paul and his wife had pledged to each other that they would introduce a male child to the religious life. Paul died when his son was only seven, but Arcadio's mother stuck to her vow. She brought Arcadio to Philibert Le Blanc, a French missionary of forty-two who had recently arrived in Fujian. Le Blanc agreed to educate the boy and prepare him for the church. Arcadio was formally adopted by Le Blanc in conformance with Qing dynasty law, and began studies under him.

Le Blanc introduced Arcadio to Catholic theology and to the Latin language. After three years he unaccountably passed the boy on to Artus de Lionne, the titular Bishop of Rosalie, who continued to train Arcadio in the same range of subjects. Probably around 1695, while in his mid-teens, Arcadio set off on a series of travels around south and central China, staying with relatives and exploring the customs of each area.

On 17 February 1702, Huang boarded a British ship at Amoy (Xiamen) and sailed for London. Only a handful of Chinese before him had journeyed to the West. His action defied Chinese law, which held that those travelling overseas were rejecting the values of their own land. An accumulation of personal factors seems to have impelled him to go: his mother had just died, his eldest sister was ready and willing to take over the management of the family, he was still restless and in a travelling mood, and he had resumed contact with de Lionne (whom he had not seen for several years) in a Fujian provincial town. When de Lionne told him he had been summoned back to Europe and suggested they travel together, Huang at once accepted. The two arrived in London in October. By late 1702 they had reached Paris and then proceeded to Rome.

In Rome Huang appears to have developed doubts about a life in holy orders. By 1711 he was back in Paris, under the employ of the Abbé Bignon, the King's Librarian. Bignon, who did not know Chinese, needed someone to help him sort and catalogue the books in Chinese and Manchu in the royal collection. Huang acquired the sonorous title of Chinese Interpreter to the King's Library, along with a small stipend.

Huang began to court Marie-Claude Regnier. He had gradually learned French, and secured translation jobs to supplement his stipend. He translated letters to and from China for a mission society, writings on astronomy and Chinese classical texts. It was a frail financial basis for a young couple, but Marie-Claude's parents seem to have liked Huang, and gave their approval for the marriage. They came regularly to the rue Guénégaud, sometimes bringing little gifts of wine and food, or making small cash loans to tide the couple over when the tradesmen's bills fell too far in arrears.

In late November 1713 the financial skies cleared for Huang and his wife. For months, the King's Librarian Bignon had been petitioning for some sort of cash payment for the Chinese bibliographer and had travelled in person to Versailles to obtain it. A firm promise for 500 *livres* was finally given by the King's Chancellor in mid-November after Bignon had used his richest rhetoric: 'Our little Chinese, for whom you have already shown some favour, has no means for staying alive other than the King's bounty . . . He hasn't a *sou*; in the name of God, give him a few *pistols* on account.' There were still a few bureaucratic hurdles, but on 27 November the sum of 500 *livres* was handed over to Huang. He and Marie-Claude at once went on a tour of all their local creditors. 'Everything is paid off,' Huang wrote delightedly in the informal journal he had begun to keep in a little soft-bound notebook. The couple at once went out to buy salt and ordered a load of firewood for delivery to their room.

Huang's thoughts turned to the future: he wanted a child. Some sense of his excitement and expectation in this period can be gleaned from his journal. His notes are usually written out in Chinese-romanized form, presumably to hide intimate details from prying eyes, and perhaps even from Marie-Claude herself. The first note, dated 11 December 1713, mentions that she had a menstrual flow a week before, during a full moon. A fertility omen? If so, the notation for 28 December is a disappointment. Marie-Claude had her period again; it had begun on the way back from a post-Christmas mass at the church of the Augustinians. Periods followed on 25 January, and in late February. Coded passages in romanized Chinese probably refer to their love-making, with Sundays either before or after mass being a favoured time.

Other notations give us a taste of the couple's life together: Marie-Claude visits the shops, the markets and the butcher; she makes a special rice pudding for Huang or his favourite fritters. As their financial status improves, the Huangs are able to acquire little luxuries: Large loaves of bread, cheeses, pâté, cakes, mushrooms. A tailor begins the fittings on a three-piece suit for Huang, to consist of breeches, embroidered waistcoat and a black top-coat. The couple love to play cards, especially piquet, with their in-laws and they regularly buy tickets for the lottery, a new institution that reflects the speculative fever of the time. There are quarrels: Marie-Claude erupts occasionally into an anger Huang cannot decipher, retiring silently to her bed and sleeping late, refusing her dinner—which Huang quite often cooked—or bursting out in a tantrum in the middle of the street. Money remains scarce and there are minor mishaps that could spell catastrophe for those on the edge of poverty: a loaf of bread missing, the loss of twenty-seven *sous*, oil spilled on one of Marie-Claude's good dresses. The couple are faithful in their attendance at mass, but Huang nearly always records them as going at different times and to different churches. If he goes to the church of the Augustinians, she goes to St. Sulpice. If he goes to St. Sulpice, she goes to St. Germain. There is a rhythm in this. Was Marie-Claude ashamed or embarrassed to be seen among the Sunday crowds with her exotic foreign husband?

But Huang had done everything possible to make himself look like an elegant French man-about-town. A meticulous clerk on the staff of the King's Library kept a record of the clothes that were given to Huang after his marriage. He lists shirts, stockings and shoes; a suit, hat and umbrella; and, surprisingly, a sword and belt. A supplementary list made by Huang himself carries finer articles: muslin cravats; frills for the sleeves of his suit, with silver buttons to fasten them; two wigs, one extremely expensive, one more modestly priced; a tasselled cane; and, most extravagant of all, a knee-length cape, buttoned down the front, of the type known as a *Roquelaure*.

As if to match his upgrading of dress, Huang began to refer to himself differently in his journal. Prior to February 1714, he had been plain 'M Houange' (sometimes 'Hoange') or 'H'. But on 8 February he is 'Mgr le Duc du St. Houange'; later in the month and into March we find 'son Eminence Monseigneur le Cardinal de Fonchan Houange', 'Monseigneur le Maréchal Hoange' and 'Mgr le Patriarche Hoange'. Marie-Claude is also promoted. One day she is 'Son Altesse serenissime Hoange' and another 'Mme la Duchesse son épouse'. His mother-in-law Regnier becomes 'Son Altesse Royale'.

In one mock grandiose passage, written on 17 February 1714, Huang wrote as if in parody of the popular novels of the day: 'So you can see, my dear reader, that Monseigneur l'ambassadeur Hoange still has a great deal to do, and has been giving audiences to all kinds of people.' The work in which Huang was engaged was the compilation of a French-Chinese dictionary, which the librarian Bignon had decided was a top priority if the royal collection was ever to be of use to French scholars. The task was extraordinarily hard, given the absence of any prior systematic study of the Chinese language in Europe and the lack of parallels between the syntax of the two cultures. To help Huang in his task, Bignon assigned him a rising young scholar named Nicolas Fréret.

A truly remarkable collaboration followed. Fréret worked steadily and patiently, during lengthy question and answer sessions, to get Huang to understand the grammatical structures that lay at the heart of the French language and that could be applied in turn to making a fruitful analysis of Chinese language. Huang's French improved under this regimen and he became able to formulate the major analytical questions himself and to provide tentative answers that Fréret would check over for him. Huang in his turn began to introduce Fréret to the structure and significance of the Chinese written characters, weaning Fréret away from the fashionable idea that they were similar to Egyptian hieroglyphic scripts.

Buoyed by mutual excitement, the two men completed a tentative vocabulary list of 2,000 Chinese words translated into French. These words were chosen for their practicability in forming simple sentences or in describing common objects and emotions. Fréret wrote in admiration of Huang's adaptability and tenacity: 'I was touched by the gentleness, the modesty, but above all the more than stoic calmness of this young Chinese who found himself in a situation that would have seemed desperate to us Europeans. Four or five thousand leagues away from home, without wealth, special skills or any help apart from a pension conditional on work at which he was sure he could not succeed alone, at which it was very hard to help him, and in which success would never be very great, he nevertheless kept an equanimity and a good humour which astonished me, and which made me believe in what various accounts have said about the Chinese character.' In a Western literature all too often replete with racist innuendoes, this is one of the grandest and most affectionate exceptions.

A Chinese living in Paris in the early eighteenth century would have been conspicuous and the object of great interest. Probably only two Chinese had visited Paris before Huang, one in the 1680s and one in 1700, and neither had stayed long. Huang was asked out often, and entertained guests at home. Among his visitors none would achieve greater fame than

Montesquieu. He was twenty-four when he visited Huang in 1713, and had just completed his law studies.

Montesquieu was planning a book that would look at French society through Asian eyes, poke fun at Frenchmen's beliefs in their own superiority and make a moral critique of European values. Though he eventually constructed the book in the form of *Lettres Persanes* (1721), we know that Huang was one of the models for the naive Persian questioners whose views turn European pretensions upside down. Montesquieu was intrigued to learn that Huang had so trusted the Christian values of the French that he had left his handsome hat in a church while he went outside for a stroll. When Huang returned, the hat had been stolen. Huang also, according to Montesquieu, had believed Europeans to be so moral that they had dispensed with capital punishment, and was amazed to find that some criminals were executed in Paris.

According to Montesquieu's record, their 1713 conversations ranged across a wide range of subjects pertaining to China: the overlapping of Confucianism, Taoism, and Buddhism; the horrors of Chinese capital punishment by burning (which was not in fact practised in Huang's time) and by slicing (which was); Chinese attire; burial practices; concepts of family property; Chinese language and grammar; the Chinese novel; the role of women and female deference; indirect address and self-deprecation in everyday life.

Montesquieu was shocked by what he learned about the mutual responsibility aspects of the Chinese judicial system, which at times required the punishment of the innocent as well as the guilty. The conversations ended—or at least Montesquieu's record of them—with a discussion of the great events in Chinese history. He wrote of his talks with Huang: 'I believe that the Chinese will absolutely never be understood by us.' Montesquieu must have revised this view, for in *De l'Esprit des Lois* (1748), his masterpiece, he includes Chinese institutions in his comparative study of political systems.

Meanwhile Fréret and Huang had intensified their work on the dictionary, shifting their procedure from arranging the entries alphabetically by pronunciation of the Chinese words, as initially suggested by Bignon, to organizing them according to the 214 groups of strokes, or 'radicals', to which the 70,000 or so Chinese characters could be reduced. But the project fell into crisis in December. Fréret was arrested for political reasons and was detained in the Bastille. The new man assigned to work with Huang, the scholar Etienne Fourmont, was a fast-rising 'orientalist' in the world of the French Academy, but also vain, ambitious and contentious. Huang was never able to form with him a friendly and harmonious working relationship, such as he had enjoyed with Fréret.

Throughout 1714 Huang was preoccupied with developments in his domestic life. In July he and his wife moved from their cramped room in rue Guénégaud to more spacious quarters on the rue des Canettes, which runs from St. Germain des Près to St. Sulpice. They bought a luxurious new bed, complete with scarlet draperies, feather mattress, pillows embroidered with yellow flowers, and jonquil-coloured taffeta covers. Huang ordered two special locks for the doors. By August it was clear that Marie-Claude was pregnant.

In the spring of 1715, Mme Huang gave birth to a baby daughter. The baby was healthy and, as a neighbour later recalled, 'looked quite Chinese, her face and colour were just those that distinguish a Chinese from a European.' But Mme Huang fell ill at the delivery, and within a few days the fever had killed her. Remembering those awful moments a year later, Huang wrote that it was as if 'God had decided, if I may put it that way, to do no more than let me get a glimpse of the wife He had chosen for me, and who was, I have to say, as dear to His heart as she was to mine.'

Huang decided not to marry again but to devote his energies to his scholarly work, and to raising his little daughter, whom he named Marie-Claude in memory of her mother. Yet his own health was worsening, his spirits were low, and the work with Fourmont went slowly. The dictionary edged forward through the various radicals, and by the autumn of 1716 had reached the 'water radical', number eighty-five out of the 214 that Huang had to cover.

Louis XIV died in 1715, and Huang eulogized the Sun King with the fervour of a patriotic Frenchman. Huang acknowledged that Louis's belief in opening the way to China had been the inspiration for his own scholarly activities. Now he would create a great work, in two volumes, that would explain everything about his native land to the French. The first volume would be largely linguistic, a grammar that would illuminate the structure of Chinese language, and explain how the written Chinese characters were able to achieve the effects made possible in the West by declension, conjugation and mood. The second volume would introduce French readers to everything they needed to know in order to gain 'an exact knowledge of the Kingdom of China', a task for which Huang felt himself well suited thanks to the wide travels he had made inside his own country before taking ship for Europe.

It was not to be. Huang felt weaker and weaker as 1716 passed from summer to autumn. He always seemed to be in need of money; for the rent, for a servant, for food, for little Marie-Claude's wet-nurse. He began to drink a lot of wine, buying it on credit. He purchased fresh eggs and milk on credit. He was writing page 1140 of his dictionary when fever overtook him. For the first time in his vast work the languages Huang had so painstakingly acquired began to blur. French words glided into Italian, Italian into Latin, Latin once more back to French. He wrote one more character, neatly, and stopped.

On 1 October 1716, Arcadio Huang died, in the rue des Canettes, leaving Marie-Claude to the mercies of the state and her grandparents. The Regent, Philip of Orleans, agreed to pay for the girl's education and upbringing if she lived beyond 1 January 1719. Until then, her grandparents would raise her, drawing on the residue—some 400 *livres*—of Huang's little estate. Huang was given a decent burial (costing forty-three *livres*) and six masses were said for his soul in October. Six more services were paid for.

Huang had hoped that his daughter Marie-Claude would live on, to embody his dream of a merging of China and France, of a better understanding between the two cultures. But she died only a few months after her father.

This essay is drawn mainly from manuscript materials in the Bibliothèque Nationale in Paris. I am also especially indebted to the published work of Danielle Elisseeff, Knud Lundbaek, André Masson and Robert Shackleton.

GIORGIO AND NICOLA
PRESSBURGER
THE TEMPLE
IN BUDAPEST

The walls had been bought by the Jews of the Teleky Market at the beginning of the century for the greater glory of God and so that they wouldn't have to cross the boulevard to get to the nearest temple. The walls had previously housed an emporium, and so appropriate works of transformation and consecration had to be carried out before the ground floor became the new temple and the upper floor became the community hall.

When I went there for the first time, a different universe was revealed to me.

The men I saw every day at the Teleky Market—haggling, arguing, toiling—were now lined up in their prayer shawls like rows of larvae. The chamber seemed vast. It was ranged with columns, pictures, lamps and galleries. I could explore only a bit at a time: the pulpit; then the part 'down there'; next what was 'to the left of the entrance'. I was never able to make a proper map of it in my head. The light was also poor, and strange apparitions emerged from the gloom. I was greatly affected by the silvered hands which shone above the Torah. I was always startled when the rolls of parchment were pulled out from beneath the vestments. I conceived of those white-clad forms as another realm of life, accompanied by a light tinkling sound, without rhythm, which I had not heard before.

The new temple of the Jews of Teleky Market had something of the Temple of Heaven and of Solomon's Temple. That such a shining light could fall upon this spot, the belly and cesspool of Budapest, seemed the work of Divine Mercy.

Occasionally, though, this world assumed an awesome face.

On the day of Kippur, when a procession carried the Torah through the temple, and at its passing the Jews covered their heads with their prayer shawls, my heart filled with terror. And also at New Year. That was when the ram's horn was blown, which was precursor of the eternal awakening in the Valley of Jehoshaphat. I would peer through my half-closed eyelids at the crowd, feeling detached, far away, among beings already dead and awaiting joyful resurrection. Sometimes I didn't even have the courage to look: I too tried to hide my head, burying it in my father's shawl, sure that within a moment something tremendous would occur, something beyond all my fears, something like the end of the world.

But these moments passed and the terrible event, the Eternal

One's arrival or an archangel's or some other representative of His, would be put off till next year.

In the temple the notion of evil, even if I had known its full significance, had no proper place. Neither the irreverences of the children, nor the reprimands that the cantor whispered to us between one verse and the next had the slightest intimation of malevolence. It was as if my soul had been protected against contrary forces or prohibitions. In the temple, I felt contentment, like a sensation, austere and deep, and it was a sensation that I hoped would last me through eternity.

Instead, at a stroke, this world was overturned.

One morning in late autumn 1944, my mother dressed me, gave me and my brothers a paper bag with a few bits of bread and roast goose, and accompanied us as far as the door of the community hall. The night before our parents had tried to explain to us that we would be quite safe in the community hall, because the King of Sweden had now bought the building and bestowed on it a special protection. The Germans and the local Nazis were, we were told, forbidden to enter.

At the door of the hall, Mother let go of our hands. A skinny woman with thick glasses took us in charge, and when I turned around Mother had disappeared.

'Where did she go?' I asked the woman with thick glasses.

She told me not to worry and to follow her. We passed in front of the temple door, but I had only a glimpse of the interior; instead of going in, we continued on up to the community hall.

We were taken to a large room whose window shutter had been carefully closed. It had two doors apart from the one we had entered by: a double door which opened on to another room like the first and a single door which led into a long corridor. The double door stood open and in these two rooms we found most of the children we played with at the temple. Although we had spent many hours together, we scarcely looked at our friends' faces.

That evening, mattresses were spread on the floor of the two rooms and some horsehair covers were thrown over them. We passed the night stretched out side by side, silently. In the morning, the woman in the thick glasses took away our bedding, and the rabbi materialized with his assistant, to give us lessons in scripture.

Gradually, however, we ceased to obey the rabbi's orders.

The menaces and severity of the Good Book seemed to us tremendous injustices. Our food was distributed at midday in milk bowls: a brownish broth made with stock cubes, and beans or cabbage. We gave up every habit, every rule. We no longer slept on the mattresses. Whoever felt tired just threw himself on the ground and fell asleep; whoever was hungry turned to the wall and ground his teeth. The latrine, accessible from the second room by a small corridor and never cleaned by anyone, was brimming with excrement. One day, tired of waiting in line, I fouled myself, standing up in my pants. I carried around this load of shit for a whole month.

In February 1945, the fighting had grown fiercer around us, and we rebelled. We had then been shut up for at least three months. That day, our cabbage soup was full of worms. Not one of us managed to swallow it. With empty stomach and trembling body, I began to cry. But it was not crying. From my throat burst bellows of protest like the roars of a bull, violent enough to shake the door and the windows. Soon my voice was joined by those of my brothers and all the other children. Ludwig Grosz—now a doctor in America—tore the clothes off his back; the bespectacled Maurer pissed on the floor; some children began vomiting gobs of stinking gall.

Like the exterminating angel the rabbi appeared among us. He silenced our cries with a stentorian shout. Swinging one arm, he knocked several children to the floor. Eyes flaming and body crouched, he flew between us, ready to break us in two. 'If he's so strong, it means he hasn't been eating worm-infested cabbage, but something better,' I thought. And perhaps I even said it, because a moment later an explosion of energy hit me in the cheek, and I felt myself swept away as if by a gust of wind. When I came to, I learned of the end of the revolt in the pale, disconsolate faces of the other children. The only concession we had won was the abolition of cabbage. From then on we were given beans.

The time came when the rooms were lacking even electric light. The lamps dangled from the ceiling; just two strips of daylight filtered through the blinds.

And then the water supply was cut off. For three days and nights we heard the shelling drawing ever closer, shaking the walls of our rooms. This was the first time that I saw fear in the eyes of the rabbi. 'We must send them away from here,' he said, not to us but to the woman with thick glasses. 'It's both just and necessary.' Soon after this we were thrust into the overcoats we had abandoned on our arrival and conducted downstairs. We were taken outside in groups. I was one of the last. I stopped dead at the door of the temple. It was the first time for ages that I had seen the light of day. I looked up and saw two planes fighting overhead: two battling angels soaring in a grey sky shaken with the thunder of the bombardment. Then, in an instant, the two angels disappeared behind the temple roof, still exchanging crimson arrows of gunfire. And a moment later an unspeakable thunder enveloped us and all the buildings around. A bomb had fallen nearby. The bespectacled Maurer and many more of my companions of those months were, at that very moment, carried off by the Angel of Death.

It was many years later when I next visited the temple. I was wandering absent-mindedly about Budapest when I came upon the street. Lifting my eyes to the peeling façade of the temple walls, I saw written in Hebrew: *Bet Keneset*, the meeting house or synagogue. I crossed over. The low doorway was not as I remembered it. I pushed open the swing-doors easily but had great difficulty in finding the right entrance. When I was finally in the temple, I felt my throat tighten. It was as if the shrinking of the Jewish population of the district had caused the contraction of the brickwork and the tiles. The place of sacred gatherings was now cramped, faded and wretched. Where were the columns? I could see only two supports in the middle of the chamber. And the benches? Many were broken and almost all had large areas of paint missing, exposing a greyish and riddled wood. Only the railings of the pulpit had been polished. The bricks of the floor were broken and cracked. On the walls dust had darkened the whitewash as if misery had sunk deep into the place.

I went up to a bench and laid my hands on it. For a moment—as though a sudden light had driven the darkness from my eyes—I saw a flock of Jews, heads covered with their *tales*, rocking themselves and murmuring their prayers; the room stretched into the far distance, and the bells of the Torah could be heard softly tinkling. 'Come and pray with us,' I heard someone whisper. I shuddered, because that voice could not be disobeyed. It was the call of the dead.

An old man came up behind me. I jumped.

'Are you looking for something?' he asked, taking at the same time imperceptible steps towards me.

I scrutinized him and felt my eyes fill with tears. It was the cantor of long ago. The man who had taught me to read Hebrew. His face was shrunken and the eyes seemed veiled. 'Are you looking for something?' he repeated.

'Uncle Stern, how are you? I'm an old pupil of yours, I murmured. Samuel Stern continued to gaze at me interrogatively. 'I came just to visit the temple!' I shouted, to overcome his deafness and suspicion.

'There's nobody here,' was his reply, 'few people come now. Most of them died, during the war.'

I shouted again, bellowing, that as a child I too had frequented that temple; he stood in front of me, perplexed. For Samuel Stern the living no longer existed, only the dead. A large piece of old stucco fell from the ceiling, breaking into dust at our feet; perhaps my shouting had dislodged it. I was startled, but the old man did not flinch.

'The limewash . . . ' he said.

I stroked his cheek with a caress before departing. I wanted to go up to the community hall, but the staircase was no longer where I remembered it. Once in the street, I realized that the upper floor now had a separate entrance and housed a state company. For me, all things considered, it was a relief not to be able to enter that room of years ago. I would have met myself a child, and that child would have asked what I had done with the rest of my life.

'I saved myself,' he would have asserted, 'and you, what have you done with the stolen years?'

Translated from the Italian by Gerald Moore

ALLAN GURGANUS

BLESSED ASSURANCE

I sold funeral insurance to North Carolina black people. I myself am not black. Like everybody else who was alive fifty-nine years ago, I was so young then, you know? I still feel bad about what went on. My wife says: Telling somebody might help. Lately, worry over this takes a percentage of my sleep right off the top. So I'm telling you, OK?

I only did it to put myself through college. I knew it wasn't right. But my parents worked the swing-shift at the cotton mill. I went through everything they earned before they earned it. I grew up in one of those employee row-houses. Our place stood near the cotton loading-ramp. Our shrubs were always tagged with fluff blown off stacked bales. My room's window screens looked flannel as my kiddie pyjamas. Mornings, the view might show six white, wind-blown hunks, big as cakes. You didn't understand you'd steadily breathed such fibres—not till, like Dad, you started coughing at age forty and died at fifty-one. I had to earn everything myself. First I tried peddling the *Book of Knowledge*. Seemed like a good thing to sell.

I attended every training session. The sharp salesman showed us how to let the 'T' volume fall open at the Taj Mahal. Our company had spent a little extra on that full-page picture. In a living-room the size of a shipping crate, I stood before my seated parents. I practised. They nodded. I still remember, 'One flick of the finger takes us from "Rome" to . . . "Rockets"!' Before I hiked off with my wares, Mom would pack a bag-lunch then wave from our fuzzy porch, 'Jerry? Say "Please" and "Thank you very much."' They like that.'

Other sales kids owned cars. I had to walk from house to house lugging my sample kit: twenty-six letters' worth of knowledge gets heavy pretty fast. My arms and back grew stronger but my spirits sort of caved in. Our sales manager assigned me to the Mill district—he claimed I had inside ties. The only thing worse than facing strangers door-to-door is finding people you know there.

Grinning, they'd ask me in. Mill employees opened their ice-boxes, brought me good things. I chattered my whole memorized routine. Neighbours acted proud of me. But I felt like a circus dog and stuffy teacher, mixed. Like a crook. When I finished, my hosts sighed, said this book-set sure sounded great. Then they admitted what we'd all known all along: they just couldn't afford it. I'd spent forty minutes ignoring this. They looked troubled as I backed out, smiling. 'Hey,' I called. 'It's copacetic, really. You'll save for the down payment. You'll get "Knowledge" on time—it'll mean more to you.' Then I knocked the next door. I stood praying for an empty house.

One day I came trudging over the mill's suspension bridge— the weight of world knowledge was giving me a hernia. My third week of no-sales. One middle-class kid had already won a trip to Mexico. 'This boy's going places,' our sales manager said. 'Whereas Jerry's going home and napping every afternoon, right, Jer?' I threw my whole kit in the river. The case flew open. Out volumes shot: *C*at through *G*raph. *U*terine through *X*anadu. All human learning (illustrated) lay sogged and ruined on the rocks below. And I loved it. I stayed to watch the current wash every book over the dam that ran the cotton mill that made the cloth that fattened accounts of the owners who'd kept my parents broke and wheezy forty years. Bye bye, Knowledge.

(In here I tried selling a vegetable-shredder. 'Make a rose out of a radish and in no time.' This is all I'll say about those two weeks of bloody fingertips and living off my demonstration salads.)

Here comes Funeral Insurance, OK, I answered an ad. The head honcho said, 'Son, I'm not promising you the moon.' I loved him for that. He was so sad you had to trust him. On his desk, a photo of one pale, disappointed-looking wife. There were six pictures of two kids shown being sweet but runty at three different ages in three different ways. I felt for the guy.

He kept his shoes propped on a dented desk. A bronze plaque there spelled: 'Windlass Insurance for Funerary Eventualities, Cleveland.' My new boss flashed me a non-personal salesman wink, he offered me a snort of whiskey from his pint bottle. I said no. I was under legal age. With Sam's legs crossed, with his eyes roaming the ceiling's water-stains, he rocked back and told. Admitting everything, his voice grew both more pained and more upbeat.

'Black people come from Africa. No news, right? But all Africans are big on funerals. It's how your tribe-people announce the respect they deserve in their next life, see? *I'm* not buying into this, understand—just laying out why a person who's got no dinner will cough up fifty cents to three bucks per Saturday for a flashy coffin and last party.

'Now, times you might get to feeling—nice boy like you, college material—like maybe you're stealing from them. You take *that* attitude, you'll wind up like . . . like me. No, you've got to accept how another type of person believes. Especially when there's such a profit in it. And remember, Our Founder was a black man. Richest coloured family in Ohio, I'm told. Plus, for all we know, they could be right, Jerry. If there *is* the so-called next world, they'll turn up in it, brass bands to announce them. And us poor white guys who sold them the tickets, we'll be deep-fat-frying underneath for ever. That'd sure get a person's attention, wouldn't it? Waking up in Hell? For being bad here?

'What I'm saying: You've got to work it out for yourself, and quick. Here's your premium book. Take plenty of change. Four bits to three bucks per week might sound like nothing to a crackerjack like you. But, with most of Coloured Town paying, it adds up. Jerry, they *do* get it back when they break the bank. Soon as some next-of-kin comes in here with the legal death certificate, I pay off like clockwork. So, yeah it's honest . . . I see that look on your face. Only thing, buddy, if they miss two weeks running, they forfeit. They lose the present policy and any other Windlass ones they've paid up. I don't care if they've put in thousands, like several of your older clients will have—if they let one, then two (count them) two big Saturdays roll by, their pile becomes the Company's.

'You getting this? See, that's the catch. I warned them during my own feistier collecting days, I'd go, "Hey, no remuneral, no funeral. No bucks, no box." They'd laugh but they got my meaning. Your client misses two back-to-back Saturdays, it's hello potter's field. Could be worse. I mean *they* won't be around to suffer through it.

'And, listen, Jer?—no exceptions to our two-week rule—none. Because, Jerry, they'll beg you. Hold firm. Way I see it, anybody who can't come up with fifty cents a week on this plane, they don't deserve the four-star treatment in the next, you know? No, I lied. That's *not* the way I see it. The way I see it—I wish I

145

hadn't washed out of dental school. The Organic Chemistry, Jerry. The goddam Organic Chemistry—I had a sick feeling about it from the first. Like a drink? That's right, you said no. So here's your book, names, addresses, amounts paid to date. See—our clients they've got nothing else—they're hoping for a better shot next go round. Your middle-class black people wouldn't touch funeral insurance with somebody else's ten-foot pole.

'Jerry, I recommend an early start on Saturday. They mostly get paid Friday night. They've mostly spent every penny by Sunday morning. And, son, they *want* to pay. So, do everybody a favour, especially yourself, grab it while it's in their hot hands. And, if you need leverage, mention . . . you know.'

'What?' I had to ask. 'Please.'

'It. A beaver-board box held together with thumbtacks. No flowers but what the neighbours pick. Not a single white-walled Packard graveside. One attention-getter is saying their hearse'll be from the City Sanitation Department. Face it: we've got a heartless business going here. And, Jer?— the minute they smell heart on you, you're down the toilet, Jerry. They'll let Number One week slide by. Then here goes Numero Duo, and they'll start blaming you. And you'll believe them. Next they'll try and bribe you—home-brewed liquor, catfish, anything. I had one woman promise me her daughter. Girl couldn't have been older than fourteen. I'm a family man, Jerry. But these people are fighting for their souls in the next life—you can understand, it matters to them. They'll do anything, anything, if you won't squeal and cut them off from their picture of heaven. But, Jerry? cut them off.

'The minute I got promoted from door-to-door, I swore I'd tell each new collector the whole rancid truth. You just got it straight-up, kiddo. Now head on out there. They'll love your Argyle sweater-vest. Is it new? Me, I plan to sit right here and get legless drunk. Hearing the deal spelled out again, it breaks me fourteen ways, it does. When I think of what a decent dental practice can net per year for a hard-working guy, when I remember certain pet clients who almost got the Full Treatment on the next plane . . . But this I'm giving you is a pep talk, mostly. It's the food in our mouths. Go, Jerry, go.'

My territory was a town of shacks. With dogs at every one. Dogs trained to attack Whitie. I, apparently, was Whitie. I bought a used car on credit. Had no choice. I couldn't walk for all the hounds—spotty small ones, ribby, yellow lion-sized things—each underfed, many dingy, all taking it extra-personally. Under my new J.C. Penny slacks, I soon wore three pairs of woollen knee-socks. I hoped the layers might soften my share of nips. I sprinted from my black Nash up on to a rickety front porch. I knocked, panting, whipping out the book. One very old woman seemed to peek from every door. Toothless, blue-black, a small head wrapped in the brightest kerchief, her shy grin mischievous. At some doorways, her hands might be coated with flour. At others she held a broom or some white man's half-ironed white business shirt. She wore male work-boots four sizes too large, the toes curled up like elf-shoes. Sometimes she smoked a pipe (we were in the forties). Her long skirt dragged the floor, pulling along string, dustballs. She asked, 'What do they want now? You ain't the one from before, you a young one,' and she chuckled at me. I smiled and swallowed.

I mentioned her upcoming funeral, its expenses, the weekly instalment due today. Overdressed for my job, I admitted working my way through college. This had melted hearts among my parents' Milltown friends. But in this zone, called Baby Africa, it didn't help.

'Working through what? Well, child, we all got to get through something.'

Some customers asked if I owned the Funeral Home. Others asked if my Daddy did. I tried explaining the concept of insurance. I failed. For one thing, my clients called it Surrance or Assurance or The Assurance. I gently corrected them. The old ladies seemed to be banking on a last sure thing. Assurance meant heavenly pin money. Shouldn't it have tipped them off, buying certainty from a confused fresh-faced kid, nineteen and about as poor as they were?

'Fine morning,' I kept grinning, even in a downpour.

'Who you supposed to be?' Some giggled, pointing at my snappy dresser's get-up, then toward a pack of mongrels waiting, patrolling the mud yard. In the seam of a half-opened door, my client's eyes would narrow. 'Oh, is you the Assurance?' It was our password and secret.

'So they tell me, ma'am,' I smiled hard. 'Yep, looks like we've got ourselves another winner of a Saturday morning going here, huh?'

The insured snorted, then eased me into a dark room I didn't want to know about.

'Seem like it's always Saturday,' my customer mumbled and shook her head. I followed her in. It was my duty to.

The same stooped old lady led me through sixty-five overheated homes. Even in mid-July, a fire burned in the grate. White picket-fencing was stacked neat, her kindling. In bare wooden rooms hot as the tropics, rooms with shades drawn, a kerosene lamp burned. Some rooms were poor and filthy, some poor and tidy, but each held an ancient woman surrounded by two dozen grandkids. Children sometimes hid when I knocked but, slowly, once I was inside, they seeped from behind doors, wiggled out from under beds. Their bellies were swollen due to lacks. They swarmed around their grannie, tugged at her long skirts, begged for treats she didn't own and couldn't buy.

The roadsides of my route bristled with zinnias, with sunflowers fourteen feet high. To my eyes, these bright, jagged hedges looked African. They seemed cut by a hand-crank can-opener out of tin. When I later learned that our white ladies' Garden Club had done the plantings, I couldn't believe it. I always figured the seeds of these plants had crossed the ocean in the warm hands of slaves chained deep inside ships.

I bought new clothes, trusting these would spiff up my errand. But Saturday after Saturday stayed a blur: kicking my dog escort, admiring the stiff flowers running defense along dirt roads, knocking on the door, sporting my brush-cut hair-do and a mail-order bow-tie, grinning out my wasted good manners on people manners couldn't save.

Windlass Funerary Eventualities Inc. had been founded in Cleveland some ninety years before. It seemed that several of my collectees had been paying since the outfit's opening day. Behind some names four completed policies had piled up. I found amazing, shameful dollar totals: *Vesta Lotte Battle, 14 Sunflower Street— commenced payment on policy #1, Mar 2, 1912, four policies complete, collected to date: $4,360.50.*

During a big rainstorm, my old Nash had its first blow-out. My parents had never owned a car, and I didn't know how to change a flat. When I bought the used sedan, I was feeling cocky, too vain to ask the salesman for instructions. Everybody else knew. I figured ownership itself would teach a guy.

So this particular Saturday morning I'm trying to collect during what seems the start of a small hurricane. I'm tooling along Sunflower when here comes a bad thumping. My Nash gimps, then tilts. I was near Mrs Battle's house but hardly knew her then. This early in my coin-collecting days, she still seemed like all the others. The good old days.

Out loud, hoping to sound like an expert, I said, 'I believe your problem is in the front-right-tire-area, Jerry.' 'No lie,' the live-in cynic answered. I climbed out. I was blinded by driving wet, dogs lunged my way, I kicked at them. Some hid under the chassis where, safe and dry, they snapped at soggy passing Argyle ankles. I took an umbrella from the trunk, lost it to wind, watched it disappear over a hedge of sunflowers whipping every which way. 'So,' I said, drenched. I unclamped the spare and a trusty jack.

I should mention that I was watched. Several dozen black faces lined up on the porches, faces interested in the weather, willing to look at anything and now all aimed, neutrally, my way. I should admit: I don't think Mr Laurel and Mr Hardy could have filled an hour with more stupid accidents than I managed in this downpour. The car fell off its jack three times. People on the porches didn't laugh outright. No, it was a deeper kind of pleasure. They shivered with it and I couldn't blame them. I noticed how one of my clients, an obese widow, had huffed her way on to an iron milk-crate. She hoped for a clearer view of my misfortune above her peonies that the wind kept scalping.

I knew that if I walked up to any of the dry people on their cosy porches and asked them for help, I'd get help. But I couldn't ask. I was too young, too proud. So I kept at it, on my hands and knees. I settled in mud, flat on my back under the Nash, trying to hold off attacking dogs by swinging a tire-iron badly needed elsewhere. When I struggled to my feet again, my own umbrella swooped back over the sunflowers and hit me in the neck. I'm still not sure that somebody didn't throw it. The spectators lifted babies. Old people in wheelchairs were being rolled out to see. I'd turned the colour of the mud, then the colour of the tires and was considering sobbing.

'Get out of the way, you.' A husky voice spoke loud enough to outlive the gale. I looked behind me. A dark old woman, scarecrow thin, hands pressed on hips, stared at me furiously. She was not amused. She seemed to hate both my incompetence and the pleasure my incompetence was giving to her neighbours. Seven blinking children, black and white, surrounded her. They were clucking disgustedly, shaking their heads.

'Don't want any favours,' said I. 'Just show me how to do this.' The children snatched my tire-iron and lug-wrench, and jerked the spare away from me. They worked around me like trained elves, the old woman snapping orders, pointing to a porch where I should stand and wait. The children had just slipped the flat into my trunk when I noticed the spare already locked in place. I studied this through slanting blue water. The dogs, tails wagging, had forgotten me and now sniffed at the children. 'How can I thank you?' I hollered over the squall—wondering if I should offer money—and followed my helpers. Then I was going up some porch steps. I worried for the old woman, soaked at her age. But she ordered, 'Get out of them soggy clothes, you.' Everybody else disappeared into the house. I was handed laundered flour sacks. I saw I should use these as towels. The children brought me a stained silk maroon dressing-robe, an antique, a hand-me-down. I changed into it, in a corner of a small front room that was stacked with consignment ironing. I dared not strip on the much-watched front porch.

Hot tea was served. I felt embarrassed. We were all settled on this strange woman's porch, we were dry. We sat sipping green tea from cups, no two alike. Everyone was silent. We could watch the rain let up or continue, it didn't matter now. My car looked clean and new. My clothes had been spread to dry in the kitchen's open oven. Sitting in the borrowed robe, I smelled like an old house.

To be with this group of helpful strangers, lined like a choir, plus the old woman, to see all the neighbours on their porches—especially the fat one next door—gaping, not at the car, but over here at our congregation staring straight out sipping warm tea, well, I felt rescued. It was a strange pleasure of the sort that makes you shudder. When rain slacked some, I dashed inside, dressed fast and backed off her porch with an overload of talky, half-apologetic etiquette that makes me cringe to recall. Soon as I got into my car I grabbed the premium book, checked her address and found the name, Vesta Lotte Battle.

The next Saturday, when I turned up to collect her regular fifty cents, nobody mentioned lending me a hand. Of course, with me being such a kid (one whose sin was and is the Sin of Pride), I never brought up my clumsiness, or their help. Me, I just let it pass. Soon everybody forgot this favour. Everybody but me.

From then on, for ever, 14 Sunflower Street was *Vesta Lotte Battle, $4,360.50.* This woman in her nineties now looked quite specific while passing me ten hand-temperature nickels at a time. I wanted to tell her, 'Look, ma'am, it's going on 1950. For the amount you've laid by, you could hire Duke Ellington's orchestra. You might get your own parade, the Goodyear blimp. Maybe even Mrs Roosevelt.'

Like other homes on my list, Vesta L. Battle's had its fair share of Jesus pictures, some of which were decaled on to varnished conch shells. But here I started noticing the unlikenesses. Mrs Battle's place was furnished with fine if ruined furniture. Possible left-overs from some great plantation house. Her andirons were life-sized bronze greyhounds. The huge horsehair loveseat had a back of pretty jigsaw curves, but one cinderblock and many bricks held up its crippled end.

She always wore a hand-me-down amethyst necklace, four of its six stones missing. Early in our acquaintance, I boldly asked her age. She shrugged, 'Courthouse burned. Someplace uphill of ninety some, I reckon.' She had cataracts. This meant that her whole head gleamed with the same, flat blue-grey colour. Like a concord grape's—that beautiful powdery blue you only find on the freshest ones. Greeting me, she stood straight. But her face hung loose off its moorings, drooping free of her like unpressed, hired-out laundry, drying, needing work. She always aimed her front toward my voice, not me. Only slowly did I understand how blind she was.

Her house milled with stray children, poor whites mixed with darker Sunflower neighbours. The first time I visited after my flat tire, fifteen were making taffy in her kitchen. They wore whole gloves of pale sticky stuff. They kept saying 'Yukk' and 'Oogh.'

Two entertained themselves with strands that slacked between them. As if in a dance they'd back apart and then, palms forward, rush each other.

Mrs Battle led me into this taffy workshop. 'Look you all, it the Boy back for Assurance.' Her voice crackled, seeming even less stay-press than her shrivelledy face. Mrs Battle's tone was smoky, flaked and layered—like the pane of isinglass I noticed glowing in her kitchen stove. She had left off ironing a white shirt. It rested, arms drooping from a board, flattened by a set of irons she had heated on her wood stove. To hold the sprinkling water, she used a Coke bottle plugged with a red celluloid-and-cork nozzle bought at Kress's for ten cents. Momma had the same one. The old woman offered me hot tea. I nodded, wondering how much she got paid per shirt. The candy-makers cleared counter-space for her.

I worried: accepting tea might be my first client-collector mistake. I hadn't asked for tire help, either. Sam warned me: 'Take nothing from anybody.' But a person can't consider every kindness to be a form of bribe. I may have been a night-school Business Major, but I wasn't *always* counting. 'Tea sounds great, ma'am.' I watched her, so old, go through the ritual. Her hands knew everything's whereabouts. This lady—I told myself, trying to keep things logical—she's in too far to ever back out of her Insurance now. She can't live much longer, can she? Vesta Lottle Battle had entered that oldness beyond plain old age. She'd hit the part where you dry out, you've become a kind of living mummy sketch of who you were. They've stopped checking your meter. Everything you could lose, you have lost. Only stubborn habits keep you moving. Like making tea. I watched her hands. They went right to each decanter, no nonsense, no waste. She'd started paying for her funeral decades before I was born. All those slow years, all these quick-arriving Saturdays.

She handed me a sky-blue teacup then scuffed deeper into her narrow home, searching for my fifty cents. Should I follow a client into her bedroom or wait out on her porch? I figured: anyplace but the yard. Fourteen dogs were waiting in the yard. Then, as always in these small houses, I felt huge and I was. Sparrow-sized black ladies kept handing their coins up to me. In a tiny wizened hand, one quarter can look almost saucer-sized.

'You children so rude,' the old voice hollered back. 'Give Assurance some eats.'

Children surrounded me, their clownish mouths caked with sugar, egg-whites. I heard Sam's voice. 'Every kindness is a form of graft.' But I smiled. The kids held their hands up toward me, wrapped to the wrists in taffy. One dark girl took my teacup, set it down then touched my hand. Over and under my ruddy right paw, she pressed her own hands, mittened in white goo. I laughed, it felt odd, though not that bad. I made a face. They hooted. I saw they'd been waiting. 'How do it taste?' a cracked voice asked behind me and I jumped. Vesta Lotte Battle made a sharp, gasping sound I later discovered to be a laugh. I smiled, held one finger to my mouth, nibbled my knuckle, 'Mmm. Thank you. It's taffy all right.'

'We knows that,' the dark girl stepped foward, ready to give me a teasing shove. Fearing for my new cardigan, I hopped back fast. They all roared. I laughed too. Somehow I didn't mind. I knew I looked ridiculous.

My hostess went back to find her money, my money. I waited in the front room. This was taking for ever. I heard two drawers open, a jar was shaken, some furniture was moved. Vesta Lotte Battle came creaking back toward me. She was bent nearly end-to-end, shrimplike. Her white hair grew in mossy, coin-sized lumps under the head-cloth. Both her hands were lifted, cupping nickels, pennies and the one dime laid, proudly, on top.

I cheerfully counted aloud for her every coin she dropped into my big clean college hand. Seemed the least I could do. But the brighter I sounded the worse I felt. Older children stopped to watch the pay-off. I felt ashamed. 'It's no popularity contest,' Sam had advised me.

Vesta Lotte Battle had paid since 1912. When she was employed as a housemaid uphill, her weekly dues ran higher. Now she had four completed policies—all ripe for forfeit if she missed just two current payments. She was into Eventualities to the tune of nearly 5,000 dollars. And on this particular taffy-making Saturday, she turned up twenty-one cents short. 'Uh oh,' I said. It was all I could think of.

'Let's see here. You had the twenty-nine but you're missing the twenty-one, correct? Look, just this once, all right, Mrs Battle.

We'll see you next week for the full amount, OK? But falling behind and all, it's just not smart. No tardiness again, all right?'

'One thing,' her voice sounded even smokier. 'I ain't no "Mrs".'

'Fine. So, we'll see you for the make-up payment next week, same time, same station, OK? But, please, have it, Mrs Battle.'

Her shoulders lifted then dropped one at a time. She said, 'Vesta Lotte Battle tries.' She let me know it was not a promise.

She stood straight, the clouded eyes now aimed right at me. Her dignity was perfect, her poise a law of nature. She closed her unpainted door. The rented hut, the tea I'd sipped, the candy, the houseful of borrowed children, the life itself, insured or not—all these were hers, not mine.

Part of my Windlass Insurance earnings paid for night-school tuition. The rest meant grocery or doctor money for my folks. I made A's in my classes but breathing was getting a lot harder for Dad. I bought him an expensive humidifier. We got him inhalers and sprays, anything.

My parents sometimes asked about my Route, as they called it. They remembered my paper-boy years. To them, my new job seemed as easy as peddling *Herald Travelers* off a bike. I couldn't explain the terrible difference. If you stop delivering somebody's morning paper, they go and buy one at the store. For Assurance, my clients couldn't turn to anybody but me. I never told my parents what the job really meant. They fretted enough. Recently I came across a snapshot of them, dressed for church and sitting on our porch. She is in his lap and laughing and they're both much handsomer than I'd let them be in memory. He wears a high white collar and has long, good hands and—except for the cheap porch furniture—these two people might be Lord and Lady Somebody, larking it up for a reporter. When I was fifteen, I gave Dad a Christmas subscription to *Life* magazine. It continued ever after, best thing I ever gave him. He wore his bifocals only once a week, when sitting down with the new issue. You'd think he had just received the Dead Sea Scrolls by mail for a first scholarly look-see. He turned pages one by one from the top corner. 'They've got pretty much everything in here,' he'd say. And if I lumbered in from work, Mom would hush me, smiling with strange pride, 'Let's be a little quiet. He's reading.'

The first time one of my customers, a retired bricklayer, fell behind in a payment and I said something stern, he wept at me, then dropped on to arthritic knees. He pressed his wet face against my creased chinos. 'Please,' I said, pulling him up. 'Don't *do* this to yourself. Nothing's worth this.' I started to see that the old folks were paying me for more than fancy burials. They were shelling out for the right to go on living another week.

I should add on the last ingredient of my Saturdays—along with old ladies (like Mrs Battle herself) and many grandkids in hand-me-downs and cornrow braids (like Mrs B's clan): about a million Jesuses.

Every ashtray, every souvenir candy-dish, baby-rattle, hand-fan (compliments of the three leading black funeral parlours), spoon-rest, pillow-cover and—once—a whole couch, showed pastel pictures of a mild-looking, soap-faced shepherd. He wore clean, pressed, 100 per cent cotton-looking robes. He had the sugar-water stare of a bad actress dolled up to play some fairy godmother. In Kress's frames, he held several sheep and one crook. I figured that maybe he gave my clients hope. Candle-white, he was shown clutching multi-coloured kids. From lithos and oleographs, he knocked on castle doors, he lifted lanterns, he carried blond infants over rickety footbridges. Promises, promises. Sometimes, alongside His picture, I'd find one of President Roosevelt, a cleaner-shaven and plumper gent but still looking like some Jesus second-cousin. Jesus places were money's most regular hiding-spots. Coins were taped behind tea-towel resurrections, tucked back of window-sized calendars that showed Christ walking the waters, his sandalled footprints denting the foamy white-caps.

Already I'd started picturing my own hands putting all of Vesta Lotte Battle's redeemed funds—a chef's salad worth of crisp green—into her outstretched leather palms, bony hands that, so glad, trembled.

Instead it was me back at her orderly shanty, smiling, 'Now, you see, you've fallen three weeks behind. We can't have this, ma'am. Really. *Three*.'

She'd brought me tea in a mended bone china cup with goldfish hand-painted on it. The saucer was a different pattern but yellow bone china too. I kept standing. So did she. Her French mantel clock, marble gilt and stopped years ago, showed a bronze blindfolded woman holding up a scale. Vesta Battle had spent her life working for the owners of the cotton mill. It showed in how she handled the tea things, how she asked, 'You wanting one lump or two, Assurance?'

'I was *saying,* "You're three weeks overdue." No sugar. Maybe one, thank you, but listen, Mrs Battle. I'm already lying to my boss. I'm paying out of my own pocket, and for your funeral, ma'am. I'd rather give you food money any day. Let's reason together, all right? Can you hear me?'

She settled across from me and stated the facts. Her eldest daughter, living in Detroit, usually mailed checks home. The last postal money-order was five weeks overdue. Mrs Battle admitted to worrying: maybe something bad had happened. And she'd never much liked her daughter's man. He fought with the line-boss at Ford. He hit Pearl way too much. Didn't seem much hope of finding what had gone wrong.

'Now we're getting somewhere!' I said. 'Just phone her.'

Mrs Battle had no phone and no number for Detroit. Besides, she didn't trust phones, never planned to touch one; if lightning hit a wire anyplace between Detroit or here, the shock would ride wires into your ear or mouth.

'Well then *write* her, for God's sake,' I said. Mrs Battle sat studying her palm's worn lines. 'Do you have Pearl's address? Let me jot it down. I'll write the letter myself. My eyes are better than yours.' She produced the Detroit address. I tore a back page from my ledger and copied it down. Later that day I mailed the letter. My tone tried balancing the businesslike with a tenderer, jokey type of lightness. Even now, at my age, I still feel superstitious about mailing certain things. Back then, too. Before dropping the letter to Pearl into the slot, I remember kissing all four corners of it for luck. I waited and hoped.

Insurance was just one of my three part-time jobs. Mrs Battle was just one of my Insurance customers. By my ninth week on the job, all my clients had broken down into themselves. There was the one missing two fingers, the one who tried to give me geranium clippings for my Mom, the plump one in the bed, the pretty young one in the wicker wheelchair, the old one in her metal wheelchair who wore a cowgirl hat, the one with the wig, the one who told the same three easy riddles each week.

I was now reading books about how to cultivate a positive manner, to make strangers do what you wanted. I learned many innocent jokes by heart. I grinned more, I switched to plain black-and-white clothes. I shook the hands of bashful kids at all my Saturdays' homes. I perspired a lot. It was a scorching September. You can't imagine the heat in some of my clients' homes.

Once, a drunk husband, who wanted the surrance money for his booze, tried to take it back. His wife helped me fight him off. 'Run,' she shouted to me. Pounding on her man's shoulders, wedging herself between him and my getaway, she sobbed at his chest, 'No! It for our Funeral, baby. Don't you hurt one flower of us two's funeral. Do, baby, and you done seen the last of me.'

I asked myself: If Life Insurance is you betting on your own death, how much worse is the Funeral kind?

Mrs Battle owed me a lot now. I was getting in over my head, and I knew it, but I couldn't stop. I considered whining to Sam. But that would mean ratting on her. I felt I should protect her. I don't know why I did. Maybe because she never explained, never thanked me. She wouldn't consider apologizing. A real aristocrat. Visiting her was like going to see some fine old Duchess in a book. At other homes I refused dandelion wine (in gallon-jugs), five free wire-wheeled tires, one lewd offer from an old man in a kimono! two dozen wonderful-smelling home-cured hams. I accepted only Mrs Battle's conversation and her green China tea. These seemed to be drudgery's one dividend. I looked forward to her face at the door. We waited for Pearl's answer to my letter, we looked forward to Pearl's checks. On Saturdays I'd save Mrs B's house for last, as a reward, almost a commission.

Sam had tipped me off: 'Once they smell heart on you, kid, you're lost.' I wondered how heart would smell to a half-blind old woman. Like beef? Like bread? Or beer? Maybe vanilla extract. How?

One windy Saturday, walking through Mrs Battle's yard, I heard a creaking in her roadside sunflowers, and I found a signboard hidden among the leaves. The wooden plaque was two feet across, and teapot-shaped. It had been enamelled pink then painted over with many black crack-marks and the words, 'CAN FIX'. I wondered, what literate person had written those two words for her? Some child, maybe. When I asked her about the sign, she pointed to a red table at the back of her kitchen. It was propped with glue pots, masking tape, brushes and, at the centre, a little scaffolding of toothpicks, twigs and popsicle sticks. A miniature ship seemed under construction. Holding my account book against my chest, I bent nearer and saw a fine old soup tureen. It looked imprisoned in its own splint. Hundreds of fissures had spoiled it but each was now caked with white powdery stuff like denture cream. Mrs Battle explained: the porcelain paste, once dried and set, would wipe off with solvent. Someday it would be as good as new. On the tureen's side an old woodland view had been daubed— quickly and with great skill. Mrs B had set little support-brads into its bowed porcelain. She'd hidden metal clips in the painted landscape; one paralleled a brown tree trunk. The brad's blue metal looked just like the tree's own shadow. You couldn't separate VLB's mending from the little ideal glade itself. I saw the beauty of the fixed tureen clearer than I would have noticed it, whole.

'It looks terrific, really,' I said. 'But will it ever hold soup again?'

'What good'd it be otherwise, Assurance? Ain't this *for* the soup?'

She seemed to consider mending a parlour game, said she'd learned it in a henhouse workshop. A lady missionary, returned from China, taught local black girls this skill in the eighteen and seventies. The final exam was: Choose one hen's egg and jump on it, then rebuild it so—to the picky naked eye—it looks unbroken. Excellent training for the world.

As I sat having tea with Mrs B, an overdressed white lady appeared, apologizing for 'having barged in'. She handed over the dust of a ruined teacup. How ruined was it? It was in one of her husband's letter-sized business envelopes.

'Ooh my my,' Mrs B laughed dry but deep. 'Somebody must've fell on this with both they boots.'

'Yes,' the woman smiled my way, 'I'm married to a man who doesn't, shall we say, have the lightest touch on earth.'

Mrs Battle sat shaking the envelope, listening to the crumbled porcelain rattle. Her face went dreamy as if she were eavesdropping on a conch-shell's pulse. 'One big mess,' she said with relish.

'Yes, well,' the customer turned to leave, 'I admit as how this may finally be beyond even your skills, my dear. But do have a go at it. Otherwise, I fear Mother's service for twenty-four is totally useless. You'll try? Good day, young man,' she nodded, maybe wondering if I'd brought VLB my busted finger-bowls. The lady stared and probably wondered why a sternly dressed young gent should be here sipping tea mid-afternoon. But I saw she didn't disapprove a bit. If anything her glance seemed jealous of VLB. So, we understood each other. Every Saturday for weeks after, I asked to see the progress of Mrs Fancy Schmantsy's cup.

First there were heaps of grit, then handle-grit, side-grit, bottom-grit. Soon they separated into Wedgwood blue and white nuggets. Shaping from the bottom up, a roundness appeared around its lower edges, the calm little sandals of picnicking gods and goddesses. I'd sometimes find Mrs B using a magnifying glass as big as Mr Sherlock Holmes's. She'd hold the cup not just near but practically against her face, pressed over her best eye, the way you mash beefsteak, to prevent swelling. She had so little eyesight left, she seemed to feel this last amount might squeeze out as a bonding glue. Once, I planned to surprise her and I stole up from behind. I heard her whisper into the cup's hollow, as into a shell or down some microphone, 'Captain Wedgwood? Coming back to you senses, sir? I setting up a meeting between you and Marse Earl Grey late next week. Won't be long now.'

Uneasy, hearing this, I tiptoed back out, and lunged in again with my call: 'Assurance!'

I liked her. My job got harder. Friday night before collection mornings, I started having regular bad dreams. I saw myself turning roses into radishes, I kept shoving people off a high bridge. Mrs Battle had fallen further behind in her payments. Three long-distance calls finally got me the Employment Office of the Ford Motor Co, Detroit, and I asked after one Pearl Battle. They found four on their payroll; what was my Pearl's middle name? I didn't know but, wait, yes I did. 'Vesta'—either Pearl Vesta or Vesta Pearl. After six minutes of crackling long-distance time (I paid, I sweated bullets) they came back, no Vesta Pearl or the other. 'Did I say Vesta? Must be slipping. I meant Lotte Pearl Battle or else Pearl Lotte Battle. Hello?' The line was dead. I went out and got drunk for the first time ever and, smashed and knee-walking, considered driving to Michigan to find my favourite's favourite daughter.

One evening, sober, headed home after my last Saturday collection (some nights it took till ten), I motored down Summit Avenue, the town's richest white street. Boys I'd known at high school were playing basketball. They were my age, these lawyers' and dentists' sons, home for Christmas break, back from freshman year at Duke, Carolina, Princeton. One goal was mounted over the big home's back door, another hung above its three-car garage. In the morning when I rode by, bound for Baby Africa, the same guys had been playing. Now, parked nearby, I slunk low in my car, headlights doused, my windows down. I sat listening to their ball pinging in that clean trusty way basketballs do. It was so dark you wondered how players could see the goals but you still heard the swish of the net, point, point. Guys horsed around; one yodelled, '*Glad I back in de land ob cotton, your feet stink and mine is rotten, look away . . .*' They called each other butter-fingers, cross-eyed, air-brain. I just sat. Lamps were being lit inside the three-storeyed house. Then the mother of the place turned on a back-porch light and came out carrying sandwiches and bottled sodas on a silver tray. She left the tray on the back step and, without a word, slipped indoors. All day these guys had been here, doing this.

I rolled up my window. I envied them, but pitied them, but mostly envied them. I drove off, slower than usual. I felt like crying. I wouldn't let myself cry. It seemed a luxury people like me couldn't afford.

I visited my night-school's tuition office. I asked for a payment extension. Six weeks only. It wouldn't happen again. I blamed family problems. That seemed true. I was paying Dad's extra medical bills, paying for household food, funding the upcoming funerals of four black strangers and one ninety-some-year-old *near*-stranger. ('If they'd just hurry up and keel over while I'm supporting them, they'd all get the red-carpet treatment.')

I lied for them. I paid. And this stupid generosity made me feel ashamed, not good like it's supposed to. I told myself, 'You're just too weak to give her up. No Princeton pre-law ball-player would be such a sap. You're helping losers, clod, because you are one.'

The Wedgwood cup, week to week, healed on her second kitchen table like a stupid, perfect, little garden vegetable. Then one day it was gone. I missed it. Back it went to its home-set, and another white person's porcelain disaster took its place. I wondered what Mrs B charged these country clubbers. Not enough, I guessed. She needed a manager.

Payment-wise, she had slipped further behind. No word from Pearl. I wondered if she'd made Pearl up, I knew better and felt ashamed, but even so . . . And yet, grouchy as I felt, I still sort of leaned toward having my tea with her. The kids at VLB's place always behaved and seemed funny, noisy in a good way. I decided not to mention how much Vesta Lotte Battle owed, not till the end of today's visit. That would spare us some embarrassment. While driving to her place, I had mapped out my speech and tactics. But once I arrived, there was something about her emptied necklace, the brocade bolsters sewn shut with clear fishing-line. There was something about how the children at her house cleaned up after themselves and looked out for each other and her. Some Saturdays when she called me 'Boy Assurance', I believed her. I wanted to. I called her 'Vesta Lotte Battle' to her face and in my head. The name started sounding classic and somehow fertile to me. But eventually I *had* to bring it up—I mean the money.

'Look, did Pearl let you know yet? I told her to write you here.'

Mrs B sat rocking somebody else's sick baby. Seven older kids, all quiet, acting groggy, maybe with fevers, rested in sweet, lost heaps around the room. My client hadn't answered me.

'Well? Are you planning to speak? I'm sorry but I'm getting cross here. I am. And who can blame me? It's January already. No word from Detroit?'

The blue-black head wagged sideways.

'Mrs Battle, with all due respect, I earn about two dollars and eighty cents per Saturday doing this. A lot of it's going to you. I've cut off some of the others. Not you. But it's plain. I can't keep this up much longer. I've carried you—week by week, I have. It hurts me but I can't much longer.'

'You ain't got to.'

Rocking the borrowed baby, she looked at me. She meant what she said. Maybe that's what always made me feel so bad. If I did drop her from the rolls, she wouldn't hold it against me. That was the absolute killer.

'Well, I know I don't have to. Not by law, I don't.' I stood before her chair, hoping she might at least offer me some tea. 'But Mrs B, you'd lose your life savings. And that's taken you your whole life to save up.'

She sat rocking, eyes aimed past me.

She seemed so unlike the others (unlike any person I've met since). How can I explain it to you? I want to. My other clients often faked long hunts for coins they knew weren't there. (Try and imagine the agony of standing before a wheelchair where an old lady in a cowgirl hat goes through every pocket of her house-dress ten times while you wait, trying to look hopeful.) Clients would hide inside their homes. I'd peek through a window and notice six adults and two children lying face-up on the floor. Caught, they'd grin, then all fake napping. 'Hi, I see you,' I'd say.

It's odd, I was standing before her chair, furious at the situation and at her, and I found myself wondering how Mrs B must have looked when she was, say, my age. By now she had nothing left but an unexplainable power. I have never bought the stuff about all old people being wise. You don't get Wisdom with your first Social Security check. I mean, here I am, near the brink of sixty and still waiting for the old light-bulb to snap on overhead. That day I saw: nothing was left Mrs Battle but a raw, quiet sureness. Mostly blind, stripped down to vitals, she could now take anything that came. Ninety some, she'd finally got limber. She could dodge it all. She could even take losing everything on my account. For that reason, I would not permit it. No.

Part of what I'm saying is: It seemed unbelievable that such a woman couldn't come up with fifty cents a week.

She asked me to go and make our tea. I did. I found I knew where she stored everything. I noted a ruined gravy boat, trying to regroup itself inside her toothpick bracings. For a second, putting water on to boil, I closed my eyes, imagining blindness, *her* blindness. I admired how she managed to fake vision. She looked right at you.

I brought Mrs B her own best one-of-a-kind cup with laurel and nasturtiums painted around it. I was pouring tea as she started talking about slave days. Uh oh. I saw her relax back into being blind. I imagined Sam scolding me, 'Jesus, kid, you just *ask* for trouble, you know that? Rule Numero Uno is: always think of your assigned list as The Group. Group Life, ever heard of it? Then everything'll go down easy as Jack Daniels. But when you start slipping, start thinking, "There's this man and that woman," then they'll really nail you, son. They know this, they plan it.' I shouldn't pay attention. History, her history, would only make me feel worse. And yet here she was, cradling the kid in one arm, using her free hand to hold a teacup to her mouth. (It seemed blind too.) Between sips, she slowly told her story. What was I going to do, mash my hand over her three-toothed mouth? Run away?

She'd been born the property of the local mill-owning family. She was freed while still a child. The day after Sherman marched through the county, burning things, the liberated slaves killed all the plantation's livestock. The old groom cut the throats of two white Arabian horses he'd curried and exercised daily. Then, knife in hand, he stood over them, crying, 'What else do I got?' She remembered everybody's dancing by torchlight in the Quarter. Ex-slaves raided their mistress's closets, wore all her gowns. Some of the little boys dressed up, tripping on hems. Freed slaves held a Harvest Ball in April, a candlelight party like ones that had lit the big house before the War. That first night of freedom, three older men asked Vesta Lotte to marry them. Freed, she now felt free to say no three times. She was eight.

Vesta Lotte rocked on, telling me of huge forest fires that Sherman's troops had set. She'd watched the town's first cotton mill burn. 'Then, right after it surrendered.'

I'd heard other older black people say, 'After It Surrendered.' They seemed to speak about some octopus, 'It', that had once had hold of them. They never said, 'After Lee surrendered.' I wanted to explain to her that maybe General Lee did finally bow out in '65, but old It had not surrendered yet.

I studied her men's work-boots, the stick-thin black ankles. On she rocked. '*Why?*' I asked, interrupting her. I got up on to my knees beside her chair, I set my cup down. I felt tempted to place my butch-waxed head into her lap beside the sick child panting there. 'Why funerals?' I couldn't help asking. How could she sink all her money into last rites? What, I half-hollered, did she imagine for herself after death? I kept still, poised on my knees beside the active rocking-chair. This was happening one quiet January Saturday on a sidestreet in Falls, North Carolina's worst possible neighbourhood. The only steady noise: squabbles among the large, black-owned dogs moping near my Nash, peeing on its whitewalls, waiting to chase me. 'Roses,' Mrs Battle answered, husky, without hesitation. 'Dozens. Roses. Thousands maybe.'

The baby in Mrs B's lap make suckling noises, dreaming. She talked on. 'And aeroplane tickets for all my grown children so's they can come on back down here for it. Around trips, too. A lined red casket be nice. Oh, and some big, white town cars, I wouldn't mind.' I understood: for her, the funeral itself was a kind of heaven. She hadn't dared picture anything more glamorous than a decent middle-class send-off. 'And marble markers with two rock lambs on top; or, if they out of lambs, maybe a couple baby angels'd do. I ain't asking much.'

I wondered aloud how many children would be heading South. 'I mean "eventually", of course.'

'Nineteen. Plus them ones what they lives with or be married to. It mount up.'

I nodded; you had to admit: the transportation costs alone could really set a person back.

We kept still for twenty minutes. I finally stood up, stiffly, feeling old myself. I cleared her tea things, brushed at the seat of my pressed pants. 'OK,' I huffed. 'But I warn you I'm only good for one more week. I know you understand how much I think of you. I've carried you, I've covered for you. I'm doing this fast-and-loose book-keeping so my boss won't nab you. But there are limits, you know, even for people like us.'

She gave me one dry shoulder-heave. The dark voice sounded: 'I reckon you'll do what you wants.'

That week I sent a final telegram to Detroit: 'Mother's Funeral in Jeopardy STOP of default STOP. Act quickly please STOP. A friend STOP.' I promised myself this would have to be the final Christian act for soft-headed, non-pre-law, thoroughly un-Princeton Jerry. My sleep was suffering, gone spotty and shallow. But I did well in my night-school business courses. I aced Philosophy but started feeling sneaky about my unnatural straight-A average. For somebody nineteen, somebody American and intending to be self-made, I was growing pretty cynical, pretty early. Funerary Eventualities had started eating me alive. On a night-school pop-quiz, one question asked, 'Define "Business Ethics".' I wrote, '"Business Ethics" is a contradiction in terms.' Then I erased this.—So I'd pass.

Life did an article about the heir to the Funerary fortune. Dad saved it for me: '*You* think this magazine is just pictures but they cover 'most everything, Jerry, what've I been telling you?' The heir, a Shaker Heights resident, was shown wearing his bathing-suit. A coffee-and-cream-toned gent, he looked plump and sleek as a neutered seal. He was a millionaire many times over, his daughter sang opera, he'd been photographed beside his Olympic swimming-pool. It was shaped like a clock, diving-boards at the twelve and six! I had to be firm. This week was it.

I rushed off to knock at Vesta Lotte Battle's door. I'd brought along a jar of my mother's excellent blackberry jam. I hoped this might sweeten and sort of humanize my bad news. I had prepared a little speech. It incorporated a quote from Plato.

I pushed open her door. No one answered. There she stood, poking her rocking-chair idly to and fro. She'd been waiting for me.

She'd sent her usual kids home. I grinned. I felt out her jar of world-class jam. I'd bought a nice plaid ribbon, I'd tied it around the lid. 'I'm afraid,' I started. 'I'm afraid this'll have to be your last free week. I believe we both knew this'd have to happen, right? From the day we met, even with our getting to be friendly and all, we've basically known it, haven't we?'

'Word come,' she fixed her ruined eyes on me, she offered me one yellow bit of paper. 'Pearl dead.'

Mrs Battle pretended to reread her telegram. She was holding the thing upside down. She was holding the goddam thing upside down. 'No,' I said. 'You made it up. No.'

I rushed over and flopped into her rocker. I held the jam against my chest, arms crossed over it, head down, bobbing back and forth in the chair, panting like my one job was to guard the jam, a bribe. 'No,' my eyes wouldn't focus right. 'A trick,' I said, 'I mean: a trick on both of us.'

I heard Mrs B step nearer, she touched my shoulder, trying to cheer me. Then her right hand crooked under my arm and she coached me into standing. She pressed her palms on the small of my back, leading me toward her overheated kitchen for our usual tea. Her head came no higher than my elbow.

I stood beside her scrubbed oak table. I set down the jam, then put my hands flat and leaned on them, my full weight tilted forward. On her mending-table, somebody's gold-rimmed fruit-bowl lay in 300 pieces.

I listened as, blind, efficient, she filled the teapot at her pump, doing everything well. I stared at the scoured table-top, saying, 'What are we going to do? Pearl was our only hope. Now we're going to lose it. Help me, Mrs Battle. Help me think this out for us. Really. Oh boy, what are we going to do here? God, what are we going to do with you?'

A dry brown hand pushed one mended, apple-green cup into my vision, a scrap of steam, a perfect cup of tea.

'Something's wrong,' Sam said. 'Black circles creeping under your eyes. You're not taking this to heart? You *are* keeping the old heart well out of this, right, Jer?'

' "Heart"?' I looked up, trying to grin. 'What's a "heart"? I never heard of one of those. "Heart"? What, is it something like a flashlight?'

' "Flashlight"! Got to remember that.' He showed me his kids' new school photos. The girl wore thick white hair-ribbons that made her thin hair look transparent. Sam kissed her picture. 'And this boy of mine's going to set the world on fire. You watch.' Sam needed my opinion about a paint colour—he planned to improve his office in two to three years' time. Nursing a bourbon bottle, he said he only drank during *our* appointments. Something about me got to him. Sam asked how *I'd* done in Organic Chem. I sat looking at this man, he might've been speaking Latin, his face looked orange to me.

Now I see I was in the middle of something like what's known today as a mini-breakdown. Then we called it the blues. We called it, Having Black Circles Under Your Eyes For A While. The Whiteboy-With-Blackness-Under-His-Baby-Blues Blues. (And the whiter the person is, the more deadly his case can be. Cotton starts out white but if you breathe white cotton for years enough, it gives you something called Brown Lung. You figure it.)

Here I'll hurry what happened next. Sometimes you rush stories because you don't have sufficient info. In this case, a person's maybe got too much. You know those memo pads with 'While You Were Out' printed at the top? Well, inside my tweed windbreaker's breast pocket, I'd recently placed just such a piece of paper. Names were written on it in my own admirable, forward-tilting Palmer script. I'd arrived at Sam's office-building early. While waiting in the weedy park across the street, I chose a sunny bench. Bored, working from memory, I copied nine offenders' names (plus their dollar amounts in arrears). To the cent, I knew. I wrote just to soothe myself, I told myself. I've always been big into lists.

How carefully I inscribed each name. Lovingly almost. One example: I traced ridges like gutters over the 'TT' in the middle of one name. I extended those crossbars to shelter the whole name Lotte. That list, hidden in my jacket pocket, crackled as I fidgeted talking to Sam. The square of yellow paper burned me like a mustard plaster.

Everybody's superstitious. About money especially. 'If I clear this figure by March, I'll give X amount to charity, really.' 'Like it or not, I'll only eat what's in the house till we go out and splurge on Friday.' The folk-ways of the wallet. Consider our nervous computerized stock market: it still uses a bull and a bear to explain itself to itself. Where money comes in, we're all primitives. Just like that, I'd carefully copied a list so I'd prevent myself from saying out loud any name on that list.

Even as I made those two T's spread like a porch-roof and guardian umbrella over the name beneath, I was giving myself one small loophole. If, and only if, Sam smelled this list on me, if he asked for it point-blank, only then might I consider letting him see it.

I'd been silent for so long. Nine old people felt they owed me their lives. Once Sam read the thing, I knew I'd feel better, I'd find the stamina to sustain Group Life a little longer. I was, after all, legally responsible to Sam and if a person's boss actually *orders* that person to hand over an inventory of backsliding wrongdoers, well . . . What can I say? I was nineteen years old. I'd been buying my own clothes since I was eleven. Other guys my age and half as smart, a tenth as driven, were already off at college, lounging around, sleeping till noon.

It was early March, Sam's office was overheated, but I couldn't take my jacket off because the list was in it. He'd know. The paper would crackle if I didn't sit real still.

My wife says: for somebody like me, somebody with a strong head for facts, it's even more important than for others to empty out the head from time to time. So I am. Clearing the books.

'Buddy? Something's off, right? College material like you, and with bags down to here. I'm seeing a wear and tear beyond the normal wear of raking in coins come Saturday. Know what Sam here's starting to think? Somebody's holding out on you, kid. You definitely got moochers. More'n one, too. Your face gives it away. You're too young to know how to hide stuff. In time, you'll get that right—but now your kisser is like neon practically. And this particular neon tells Sam, says, "Sam, certain moneys are coming directly out of young Jerry's personal bone-marrow." You got parasites, Jer. It shows. Draining you.

'You're shielding them but who's looking after *you*? Your folks? Naw, you're on your own. I'm here for you. You were handsome when I hired you. *Now* look. Your pant cuffs are frayed, the boy can't even sit up straight. Jerry, who you covering for? Let me help, son. I swear it won't get past this desk. You know their names; you maybe even wrote names down. Yeah, probably got those tucked somewheres on your person. Look, kid, trust me here. You want Sam to step around his desk, ease you against that wall and frisk you, Jer? You're a good-looking kid, Jerry, but not that good. Spare us both. Pass your Uncle the names. I'll need the exact dollar amount each leech has sucked out of my favourite. Jerry? Tell your Uncle Sam.'

Tears stood in my boss's eyes. That's when I knew I had to let him save me. Yellow is such a beautiful positive colour, isn't it? *While You Were Out . . .*

I slept well that night! Why lie about it? I dropped off saying things like 'Figures don't lie.' It was a sleep too deep to let one single dream tax it, just blackness so pure I woke up sweaty, half-panting. Getting true rest seemed the most exerting thing I'd done in months. One room away, Dad coughed, Mom promised him it would be all right, she pounded his back, Dad thanked her, he said it had passed, he choked again.

The Friday after, I was driving toward the night-school business office to make my overdue payment. I had got certain bonuses and could again fund my education. I still collected for Windlass but now avoided the 200 block of Sunflower Street. I called on that block's paying clients only after dark. It was a gusty March afternoon, dust devils spun along the roadside. Winds rocked even the biggest trees. One wad of cotton, large as a hassock, came tumbling down the centreline, rolled up on to my car hood and snagged one windshield wiper. I braked, cussed, got out to yank it off and, 200 yards away in Baby Africa's clay cemetery, saw a funeral in progress.

Women were hunched under shawls, men held hats against their chests. Everybody, fighting the wind, kept faces turned down and aside. They all looked ashamed and, in my present state, this at once attracted me. An old woman stood surrounded by kids. 'It's

Pearl's,' I said. 'They're burying Pearl.' My voice broke. Please understand I am not asking for credit. I slunk back into my Nash, flipped down both sun visors, prepared to roar off. Then unexpectedly my car was pulling over, I was out in the air, was walking toward a familiar group. Like so much I did back then, I hadn't planned to do this. I remember dry weeds snapping under my new loafers. I waited, off to one side, hands joined before me. I was the only white person present.

Two weeks back, I had made four phone calls to the Detroit morgue; I had helped to get Pearl's body shipped home in a railroad ice-car. The trip had taken eleven days. Pearl's coffin was splintery pine. You could see black nail-ends bent crooked under half-moon hammer-dents. Must have been the crate they packed her belongings in. Somebody had tried painting out stencilled instructions: *This Side Up. Keep Refrigerated At All Times.* Near the coffin's tapering foot-end, a Maxwell House Coffee can rested on the ground. It was stuffed with dried hydrangea blooms as big as human heads. Alongside the jagged grave, a pile of earth waited. Wind kept flicking dirt off the pile and on to the mourners. Everybody stood with eyes closed, in prayer and to protect themselves from the flying grit.

People lined up to look into the coffin a last time. I had never seen an open coffin at a graveyard. But I felt I couldn't hold back. When I joined the line, Mrs B's neighbour-kids saw me. They suddenly closed ranks around her. Only then did she turn in my general direction. Her neck lengthened, the blue-grey head twisting my way. I knew she couldn't see me at this distance but both VLB's arms lifted from her sides. She seemed to be hearing a sound or maybe scented me. I felt honoured, weak.

The woman in the box was over seventy. She wore a mostly emptied amethyst necklace. On her chest a gold pin-watch read FORD MOTORS, a prize for perfect attendance. Her age shocked me. I'd always pictured Pearl as just a bit older than me. I now saw: that would've made Vesta Lotte Battle a mother at seventy-three or so.

In the makeshift coffin, Pearl's head had shifted to one side; she faced pine planks like a person choosing to look punished, refusing even a last chance at formality. The coffin was closed, boys nailing it shut. The nails kept doubling over and this looked ugly and grieved me. Strong young boys lowered Pearl's crate by ropes. Mourners started heaping up the dirt. They had brought garden spades and shovels from home, and there was no professional grave-digger.

The girl who'd once pressed my hand between her candied palms now led Mrs B away, detouring to avoid me. I approached them. I was helpless not to. My mouth and lips felt novocained (I later realized I'd been mercilessly biting them without knowing it). I felt foolish and exposed. But I still needed something from the old lady. *My* old lady, I thought of her, but knew I had no right.

She must have seen a pink blur fumble nearer. VLB resisted ten children who tried dragging her past me. When she stopped, the kids eased back, but their chins stayed lifted, hands knotting into fists. I didn't blame them. I knew how I must have looked. I kept swallowing to keep from smiling; I gulped down a beefy-yeasty-copperpenny taste that turned out to be blood.

Mrs Battle, grieving far from her familiar house, seemed disoriented. Her skin had lost its grapey lustre; she now looked floured in fine ash, her eyes too. Daylight showed a face composed entirely of cracks depending on splits and folds; her hands stayed out in front of her, long fingers opening and closing, combing air. She groped my way, lightly, almost fondly. Plain daylight showed her to be tiny, malnourished maybe. The sun made her look like a blind person. I have to say: it made things easier on me just then.

She faltered quite close, finally touched my sleeve, but jerked back as if from a shock, 'Ah,' her voice recognized me. 'You, Assurance?'

'Yes ma'am,' I studied my new shoes.

'You did come. I knew it. I done told them. And we thanks you. Pearl'd be glad. Look, not to worry 'bout all that other, hear? We doing just fine. Fact is, been missing you more than we miss it, Assurance. You steadily helped me to find my Pearl, get her on back here. Don't go fretting none, child, you tried. You gone be fine. I'm gone be fine.' She turned and moved away from me supported by the children's spindly arms and legs.

I waited till everybody left. The wind got worse. I stood at Pearl's grave. Hand-prints and shoe-marks had packed the earth.

Wind had tipped the coffee can. Water made mud of the grave's foot-end. I squatted and crammed hydrangeas back into the tin and set it upright. Last year's hydrangeas had dried brown but still showed most of their strong first blue. You know the colour of hydrangeas, that heavenly blue so raw it comes close to seeming in bad taste.

I drove out into the country and passed a rural mailbox I'd always admired and meant to examine. I did that now for no good reason. It was a life-sized Uncle Sam enamelled red, white and blue, and meat-pink for his face and hands. The eyes were rhinestone buttons salvaged off some woman's coat. His vest-buttons were dimes glued on and varnished. While I stood looking, the proud owner stepped out of a tractor shed then headed over to tell me how he'd got the idea and to accept my compliments. I panicked, saw myself as one of those guys, like Dad, who'll jaw for forty minutes with complete strangers over nothing. I hopped back into my Nash and squalled away.

I drove to Joe's All-Round Store, to buy staples for my folks. Mom loved angel-food cake. With a little teasing encouragement from me, she could sit at our kitchen table and pull off one bit of white fluff at a time till she'd eaten it, whole. The embarrassment was part of her joy. 'I *ate* that? *I* ate it all?' And somehow she never gained. So I got her a big Merita angel cake and, for Dad, the Giant Economy size of Vick's Vap-O-Rub. (On his worst coughing nights, he sometimes dipped one finger in and swallowed gobs of it till I had to leave the room.)

I dropped off my folks' supplies, explaining I was headed for the public library to hit the books. Instead, pretending to myself I didn't know what I was up to, I drove along Sunflower, switched off my ignition and headlights, and coasted to a halt three houses down from Mrs Battle's.

I sat screened by dried sunflower-stalks creaking in the breeze. I looked toward her kerosene-lit home. Children were in there talking, a wave of laughter broke. Her narrow body, half-doubled, criss-crossed the room from ironing-board to stove and back, for tea, for hotter irons. I knew hers was just a little bent black nail of a body, but she threw large blue shadows. I slumped out, feeling like a spy or a spurned lover, like some hick planning a stepladder elopement. I knew if I walked up and knocked at her screen door, she'd say, 'Look children, our Boy Assurance's back.' The children might act snooty but she'd make tea for me in a mended cup so fine you could hold it up and read its maker's name imprinted on the bottom, even against a kerosene lantern's glow.

Why was I waiting? Did I hope she'd sense my presence and suddenly pop up as she did when my tire blew? Maybe I could take her for a car-ride tonight, find her and the kids ice-cream. On me, of course. I could send her two cords of firewood. I became disgusted with myself and drove home. I stayed up late, studying. I didn't get much time for schoolwork during the day. I had a couple of other jobs: I managed a soda fountain and, after hours, cleaned two laundromats for a hermit bachelor who owned much of Falls and spent nothing.

Late that night, I heard Dad hacking in a new way, more shrill, yappier. I stood up from the card-table that was my desk. I eased along our short hall and waited outside my folks' room. The cough came again. Only, it was my mother coughing. Her case had never seemed as bad as his. Whenever Momma got to hacking, she laughed, claiming it was a kind of sympathy vote for *his* short-windedness. They'd worked cleaning the same looming machines for thirty-some years. Why did I believe she had found a purer air supply than his? I assumed that Dad, after thirty-seven years, had pulled enough fibre into his plugged lungs to weave a long-sleeve shirt with. But Mom? That night, I found she'd inhaled enough to make one lacy, deadly blouse. I stood listening, though this meant asking for more trouble.

Six weeks after the Detroit police wired news of Pearl's death, two weeks after Pearl's burial, I was driving Sunflower, still collecting. I'm half past Vesta Lotte Battle's clean shanty when I see a fresh white wreath nailed to her front door. Poor Pearl, I thought. Lined along VLB's weathered porch, a dozen children, black, white, brown, all wearing play clothes, all sitting still. They were eating the usual pale taffy, but were gobbling it down like a group poison. Two slow blocks and a thousand sunflowers later, I understood: the old lady was dead.

I drove on, forgetting waiting clients. I speeded right through town, hands choking the wheel. A hypodermic had just wedged under my breastbone, sucking, leeching out my breath. The roadway was turning yellow from the edges inward and I finally pulled over and parked in a field. A meadowlark balanced on a cat-tail gone to seed. And all at once I remembered how to breathe. I sat in the Nash gasping like a diver who's just found the surface, his life again.

I found out that Mrs Battle's funeral had been held two days before. I decided to attend another black funeral. I checked Monday morning's *Herald Traveler* for a likely name and church. I called in sick to my laundromat-cleaning and soda-jerk jobs. I'd never done that before. The church I picked was just off Sunflower Street. I had to drive right past the Battle home. A 'For Rent' sign was already staked into her front yard. Browned sunflowers had been cleared, the hanging enamelled teapot was gone. I hoped that Vesta Lotte Battle's kids would claim the thing before some realtor removed it as an eyesore. Real-estate agents didn't waste any time, the blood-suckers. I kept trying to forget my parents' new calibre of rattling. They now seemed to alternate the need to breathe—him then her, her then him—like taking turns, waiting for each other's pleasure.

My '39 Nash coasted to a stop before the ramshackle church. The Afro-Baptist Free Will Full-Gospel Church appeared bandaged in three kinds of tar-paper brick. Its roof showed crude, dribbled asphalt mending. One unpainted steeple tilted. The place looked as home-crafted as some three-tiered dollhouse, doghouse or out-house. Even in early April, church window-boxes spilled great purple clouds of petunias. From one box a sunflower had sprouted out of a wind-blown seed, and though it looked totally out of place, it had already lifted a few feet high, straining toward the rusty gutters.

Parked in one low, Hollywoodish line, hired white limos gleamed with sunlight, hurt my eyes. An empty hearse bloomed big ostrich plumes and small American flags from its silver fenders. Black morticians loitered in white suits and dark glasses. The undertakers smoked, polished their cars, stood in proud, jumpy groups. They acted like Secret Service men outside a civic building where some bigwig official is appearing. They waited, smug and antsy, for their boss: today's highest-paying black body in Falls, North Carolina.

I was one of three whites in a large, loud congregation. I kept straightening my black tie. Elders welcomed me with a great ceremony and graciousness that made me feel even more a worm, a spy. Why was I here? To pay respects. Came time to view the corpse. Almost immediately it happened, people filed toward the box. All the people in my row stood. Somebody nudged me from the left. I rose, not quite meaning it. In drill-like formation, we marched toward the knotty-pine altar and the coffin propped over velvet-draped saw-horses.

It was a Monday. I had had my premium book and a few rolls of quarters in my car's glove compartment, left there from Saturday rounds. I didn't want to leave them outside in that neighbourhood (being the neighbourhood where I collected), so I brought them into the church. I carried them when I approached the open coffin. The insurance ledger was imitation black alligator, hinged so it flipped open like a paper-boy's record book. It bulged in my jacket pocket. I took it out and held it, hoping it would pass for a prayerbook. I was sweating, and nearly dropped the slippery thing. I grabbed at it, gulping. I imagined my list of names toppling into the box.

She looked to be about thirty-eight. All in lilac, a cocktail dress. Pinkish feathers curled around her head like a night-club idea of a halo. Her coffin was lined in white glove leather, the sides were plugged with gleaming chrome buttons; it was framed in oiled walnut, and smelled like a brand-new Cadillac convertible. For a moment I wanted to climb in. I don't know why. I hadn't eaten much that day and was giddy.

The stranger's chest was massed with purple orchids. Flowers picked up the exact colour of her dress. I wondered if the orchids might be painted. But I could see that they were real. Huge, curling bugle-nosed orchids seemed to crouch on her breastbone, guarding her and feeding on her. Above her coffin, along the empty choir-loft's edge, there were dozens, maybe hundreds, of Easter lilies.

The lilies washed Afro-Baptist with a sweet smell that burned my sinuses and eyes.

Returning to my seat, I heard quarters jingling. A roll was unpeeling in my pocket. I winced. Trying to tamp the sound, I grinned.

The huge choir swooped into place. Lined up like a jury, they nearly outnumbered the mourners. They arrived singing something called 'Blessed Assurance'. The appropriateness of the hymn changed and deepened from verse to verse: what was a wild coincidence became almost expected, natural.

The small children in the choir sang out behind spiky white lilies. Some of the kids might have been among Mrs Battle's household regulars but I wasn't sure. (When a boy is nineteen, all little kids look alike.) Over the flowers you could see the dark, cloudy hair of the tallest children, their heads tipping side to side as their mouths moved:

> *Blessed Assurance, Jesus is mine!*
> *Oh, what a foretaste of glory di-vine!*
> *Heir of salvation, purchase of God,*
> *Born of His Spirit, washed in His Blood.*
> *This is my story, this is my song,*
> *Praising my Saviour all the day long.*

I felt drunk, half-faint. I'd settled near the back. I could only bear to watch my own pale hands. I studied the wrists' yellow hair shining in the daylight. I thought odd things; 'Strange, how no American coin is gold-coloured.' I looked at my long fingers' freckled backs, I turned over my wet pink palms. My hands seemed to belong to one plump and silly boy. But my eyes, staring down from what felt like a great and sickening height, seemed the eyes of an old man teetering at the brink of a cliff.

Everything seemed swollen past proportion, quantum. The choir members turned in place, and as they spun around their white sleeves flared like cheap wings. The choir-loft was stair-stepped in rows. At any moment three or four singers would be whirling, their robes cheerfully slapping the robes of those beside them.

At football games everybody in your bleachers starts leaning side to side and shouting one thing—it was like that now. The choir considered us the winning side.

I fought the congregation's rock and sway. I considered leaving. I felt out of my depth. But I knew that in climbing over six weeping strangers singing on my pew, I'd have to say, 'Excuse me. So sorry. Thank you, oops, pardon.' So I fought the tilting. Everybody moved but me. I now turned into a blond, chilly Princeton boy. The volume grew. They were working on me. Everyone sang in three-part harmony, like conservatory graduates, skilled, and with perfect diction.

Bumped from either side, I muttered at the woman beside me. Cheerful behind her tears, she yelled, 'Tell it, bro!' I explained how a person could use a little more room. She nodded. My complaints seemed to swell the hymn. I surrendered and joined the singing.

Our group stopped in one ragged rush. I was loud, alone, off-key for one long second. I sucked air, swallowed 'Fool!', curled my toes. People were standing up one by one. Fanning themselves with Jesus fans, they talked about the corpse.

'She been a mighty good neighbour, Lila,' the woman near me rose. 'One time, remember when my William cut his foot so bad on that soda bottle? Well she look after all my other little ones the whole night till we walk back home from the Doctor's out Middlesex way. Then Lila say, Don't you be coming in here waking up these babies in the middle of no night, you let them sleep. She kept mine over to her house till they all awake and then she fed them a mighty fine breakfast, sent them back on home to me. Too, Lila done give my momma eighty cents, one time she couldn't pay.'

'Lila,' one old man with two canes called. 'Had the prettiest yard on Atlantic Avenue, better'n mine and you know how nice mine is. Yeah, she got her dahlias to someway grow big as you head. Used bonemeal, some says.'

They told why she never married (she tended her sick mother). They said she dearly loved a moving picture show. She knew the age and facts of every movie star on-screen. Lila's say-so settled every movie bet or argument in Baby Africa.

After the testimonies, the music started again and I threw myself into the pump and swell of hymns. The preacher on his varnished perch interrupted: 'We hopes our white friends will feel free and speak.' He bared his square white teeth in a smile for the first and only time that day. A lone white lady popped up and

177

looked around nervously. She was forcing herself. I felt for her as she cleared her throat, stranded and alarmed, but determined. She wore trim navy-blue, her foil-coloured hair in a knotty permanent. I couldn't place her name but, knowing Falls the way this ex-paper-boy did, I could've told you her street address to within one block.

In a girlish voice, the lady said she had hired Lila for many years. She admitted how hard Lila had worked, far above the call of duty. She sounded short of breath. You could hardly hear her. Everybody tipped forward, trying to hear. 'Feel we never . . . understood or whatever what a fine person . . . we had . . . around our house till Lila got so . . . so sick last . . . June was it?' she turned to the man seated beside her.

'June, yes. Lila'd fallen in our rec room. We came back on Monday. We found her. She'd knocked over liquid floor-wax and was lying in it, it'd dried. And when my sons pulled her to standing, the sound was like the flooring coming up with her. She was embarrassed about having spilled. It was too awful. The first Monday she didn't turn up for work, I felt our house was like . . .' the lady paused, 'like . . . house . . . was . . . hollow. There was an echo, it seemed all our rugs had been taken out. My husband can tell you. Now it seems that . . . to be . . . our self—our best selves— we needed Lila there to . . . And since she . . .' She curved one palm around her throat, gulping, unable to find a voice. But she did not sit down. Her husband reached out to touch her back, decided against it—straightened his own posture instead. The woman wanted to sit—she knew people would forgive her. But she'd decided to finish.

'Tell the truth,' some old man called, rapping floorboards with two home-made walking-sticks. 'Jesus going to see that you get all the air you needs for speaking true. Jesus going to fan some cold truth-telling wind down into you. You watch.'

The woman smiled back at him, nodding. Her fist rapped her sternum, she shook her prim head sideways. Her embarrassment, I saw, was a country club white person's. Social embarrassment. She feared she looked foolish. *Being* foolish pained her less than getting caught at it by strangers, especially decent black ones. I felt for her. Takes one to know one. The Black-and-Blue-About-Being-White Blues.

'Loving Lila,' the white woman tried summing up. 'Might've let us love each other more, but I'm not sure that was reason enough . . . for taking up her life the way we did. And by accident almost, looking back. We gave her ten days off a year. Five of those she spent at the beach house with us. She cooked for us there. Which was no vacation. I see that now. Believe me, I'm living with this. We learned so much from her. Look, we loved her is all. Maybe that's the best thing you can teach anybody? I don't know.'

She sat down, face in hands. 'Amen. It'll do,' somebody shouted. Heads bobbed.

The white man hopped up to remark that what his wife had just said went double for him.

Then I stood. I hadn't known I would. Suddenly the church had sunk and left me vertical. I think the singing had made me light-headed.

I told everybody I felt real bad about selling funeral insurance. I told why I'd come. I admitted seeing the great beauty of the ceremony. I conceded: Negro funerals had it all over white ones—much more personal and everything. But it seemed I'd never understand enough to help me feel quite easy with the business end of burial. I admitted that some of my most beloved clients had lapsed. I'd let them drift from the black into the red and then I told on them. I couldn't rescue the whole world, though for a while I'd given it my level best. You try and save a drowner, but if you drown too what good is that to anybody? Sure I wanted a college education but not one built by walking on the heads of others. I apologized for taking up their time with something not exactly on the subject. Then I added—I knew it was feeble—that Miss Lila's lilac dress was about the finest-looking lilac dress I'd ever seen. 'Amen. Ain't it, though?' two old women, maybe twins, hollered. I sat down, breathing hard. There was no way I would start sobbing like a fool, not with everybody looking. The old man up front started beating the floorboards with his canes. He cried back at me, 'Jesus Have His Ways, Child. Be of Comfort, Son. You going to act right. You wait. Scales going to fall off them young eyes by-and-by. You'll see.'

I knew what I had to do.

I stood up again. I emptied my pockets of all rolled quarters and loose change. I yanked out every bill. I whipped the premium book from my jacket.

Mourners between the aisle and me kindly slid out. They let me step free. I walked to the tin collection plates tucked behind massed lilies. Into one plate, I piled all my money. About eighty-nine dollars and fifty cents, I think.

Then, into another plate, I dropped the keys to my loyal Nash. I said where my car was parked, what kind it was, what colour. 'Oh Lord,' somebody called. 'Jesus got them Miracle-Working Ways. He look into the whiteboy Soul. He Clean House.'

I announced that I wanted some kind of college scholarship set up. It would help some straight-A child from the church. Elders could sell my used car—that, and what cash I'd left, would at least help get things rolling. The fund would be named to honour . . . Miss Lila. I didn't want to say Vesta Lotte Battle's name. Then they'd know it was me that turned her in. I left.

Two ushers swung open the exits for me. One young man was smiling, face all wet. The older gave me a 'Who are you kidding?' stare, his mouth was big, postcard-sized and folded in with scorn. His reaction seemed right. But as soon as the sun hit me, I felt light and wonderful. Sunflowers and zinnias seemed my African honour guard. I was weightless for six blocks.

I walked back to my parents' place. They hadn't heard my car and asked what was wrong, where I had parked. I told them about the funeral. They sat looking at each other. Dad's latest *Life* rested open on his lap. I remember Ava Gardner was on the cover. She's also from North Carolina, from very much the wrong side of the tracks and with the face of a Contessa and I have always loved her. My parents could not drive. They called my Nash 'Jerry's runabout'. I would take them shopping in it or out to the Dairy Queen.

Finally Dad laughed, removed his glasses, folded them. He had an uneducated person's respect for eye-glasses, as if they were a substitute for a college degree. He set them in their little casket, snapped it shut. Shaking his head side to side, he told Mom, 'They give our boy free encyclopaedias, he throws them in the drink. Now he's gone and handed over his roadster to the coloured people because *they're* poor. Who knows? Maybe if a boy acts like a rich man long enough, he turns into one? Sure hope so.'

Then his chuckling slid, as always, right down breath's stairsteps into deep and deeper coughs till you never thought his wind would surface again. Mom jumped up and stood patting his back. That never helped but he liked it anyway. Momma bent toward me, bent across Dad's leatherette easy-chair. She touched the top of my hair, then one side of my neck. 'Jerry's always had him a soft streak,' she said.

'It's not soft,' I snapped back. 'It's hard. It's the only part I like. The rest is sloppy and extra.' She pitied me, knowing I was weak enough to pity others. I hated her for that.

I stumbled to my room, threw myself on to the bed, mashed my face into the chenille spread's nubbins, pretending they were Braille and that I would read what to do next. I wished I hadn't left my premium book in the collection plate. I worried what might happen to my other clients. Even with Mrs Battle gone, I still had big responsibilities. My ledger was the only record for the thousands of dollars that older folks had saved toward their standing on the next plane. Would they miss out on their hard-earned heaven just because I'd lost my head while feeling generous?

Two days later, the mailman brought me a package. In it, my insurance book, all the money I'd left, plus—held to a piece of cardboard by criss-crossed electrician's tape—my car keys. The cardboard said, 'Parked right where it was.' A note read: 'We all get move sometime. Sometime we needs to think out why. If it still the same way you felt then we start up the college thing for one our young folk. If not then that OK too. Cause we all Children OF God. Either way you a man of heart. IN Christ Blood Bartered for us sinners I am Rev. T. Y. Matthews—Free Will Afro-Baptist (Church).'

I sat down to write a cheque for 200 dollars. It was the largest cheque I'd ever written. My hands shook. I kept the ledger. And I collected the car. I waited till night to get it. I did not want to be seen. My parents applauded when they heard me pull up. 'Pile in,' I hollered and they came running like kids rasping from a touch of croup. I drove them to the Dairy Queen. They sat in back, royalty, holding hands. We said nothing the whole way out and home. They were back there, sighing, eating their cones. As I drove I breathed through my mouth, not wanting to cry. The three of us, we had been so unlucky, really. Getting back what little was ours seemed a great reward.

I drove to Sam's office the next day, I meant to turn in my book and quit. But just outside his door, I decided to collect for two more weeks. I'm not sure why. I suppose I wanted to get things cleaned up for whatever poor soul Windlass Eventualities hired next. Two more Saturdays.

Again I knocked. Mrs Battle's neighbour, a hugely fat widow, peeked out. She said, 'You come for your Assurance? Is you new? You look older than that last one.'

'Yes ma'am, older.'

From inside the darkest corner of her home, underlit by a dime-store votive candle, a Jesus grinned. He was dressed in powder blue and white, beard marcelled just so, and he had a twenty-four-carat halo. He looked guilty over being so pretty on a street of such need. The client's payments were only two weeks overdue. She'd greeted me with a broad face so scared I didn't like to see it. Dead Lila in her box looked much more in control than this living woman did. 'I checks,' she shook her head, 'I goes and looks but I real low just now.'

Watching her move, I wondered how somebody so poor could be so mammoth.

She lumbered toward a tiny vase that showed another Jesus hammocked among clouds, arms out like a diver about to leap. The vase sounded empty. She stood with her eyes closed, one ear mashed against the vase, like someone listening to a seashell.

'Seem like it ought to be around here.' The widow moved from vase to firewood box to mantel. She shifted things. I saw an unopened jar of jam, a tartan bow topping it. A gift from Mrs Battle?

'I busy checking,' the woman promised.

I remembered Mrs Battle's words: 'I ain't got no money today.' 'Pearl Dead.' 'Vesta Lotte Battle tries.' 'You'll do what you want, I reckon.'

'Maybe it been stole. Yeah, stole probable.' The obese woman patted around behind a sheeny Last Supper wall rug. Then she moved to a calendar that showed Christ holding out his own lit-up and dripping heart. His face looked sober.

'Assurance? These young boys now'll steal you blind. Ain't nobody safe. Too, I getting so I forgets. You sure it already

Saturday again? I done sunk mighty low but I still hunting. Don't
you fret your pretty head none, I gone find it yet. You so pretty.
Look how good and yellow his hair is. Golder'n that,' and she
scanned the room for her favourite picture, then pointed to the
rouged Jesus who posed nearby—heartless himself because He
kept offering things to everybody.

Her flattery sickened me. 'Here,' I said, bending and kicking
up one corner of her rag rug. Since the house was dark, since her
notched swollen back was toward me, it was easy to unpocket the
two quarters. I picked them up, held them out to her. 'These?' I
said.

She turned and made a cry, 'No!' She inched forward, blinking,
her jaw slack. Each huge arm lifted from the elbow, wobbled like
udders as she neared me. The sad weight hanging off her sides and
breasts suddenly seemed like a burden that had been assigned.
In her face, surprise mixed with fear, fear that I meant to trick her. I
couldn't stand watching. *May this job end, and now, Amen. I am not
fit to earn a living in this world.* 'So let's see here, that's fifty—five-
zero—cents, paid in full.' I fiddled with my black book, 'Listen,
there'll be a new fellow next week. Just to make sure you get full
credit, you'll want to save these. Just give him these next week,
OK?'

I passed her fifty cents. All the hut's accidental sunlight, and
the shine from her red candle, got snagged across two silver coins.
Her calloused hand, charcoal dark on its back, showed a pale pink-
copper colour inside. It seemed that years of work for whites had
rubbed the black pigment off her palm.

Her face gleamed, her upper body rocked toward me.
Moaning, she showed me my own coins as if they were two working
eyes that some genius had awarded a blind woman, that she could
pop right into ruined sockets, and see again.

'I still on the assurance, Assurance?'

Beside her name, I read the tally, three policies complete: two
thousand three hundred five dollars and fifty cents. 'Consider
yourself carried, please.' I backed into daylight, glad even for the
posse of sunning mongrels. They rose, stretching, grumpy at their
duty. We all have our jobs.

She hid both eyes behind the heavy crook of a great arm.

I heard her weeping, then explaining to the crowd of paper Jesuses, 'Your Dorothy ain't lost out after all, Saviour. You done carried her over into the Promised Land of another week of Surrance and for free. I still under the coverage. Your old Dot here, she still covered, Lord.'

N ow I'm going on sixty. The years are really the bottom line. I'm semi-retired, I've had the usual two heart attacks but I got the best cardiac specialists, so I lived. As a young man I went into business for myself. I actually did pretty well.

It came about in a strange way. I was working other odd jobs, saving up for law school. I'd earned my BS through night courses. My parents lived to see me graduate. They were so happy about it. My father wore his reading glasses all through the ceremony. I wanted to tell them, 'No, this is just the start, don't be so thrilled so early.' But they were.

I wonder what they would think if they could see where I live now. We just built a fancy guest wing on to our beach place. I designed it myself. It doubled the floor-space of our original cottage. These days we don't have too much company and the addition is not very practical, but I wanted to add it on anyway. The kids come down when they can get away from their jobs and such. My wife calls the wing, with its white spiral staircase, its glass, its cathedral ceilings, Gerald's Taj Mahal. My wife is from one of the old families around here. She stops short of calling my new annex that dreaded word of hers: 'nouveau'.

Last August, she and I were sitting on our new porch, reading. It was late afternoon. A young white couple, strangers, wandered off the public beach. Holding hands, they crossed our property and headed toward the road. They were country kids in bathing-suits, very tall, and they moved well; they were as good-looking as they would ever be. They walked right by the entrance to our new guest wing. I jumped up. 'What's wrong?' Millie asked from behind me. I shook my head and didn't answer for a while. In that moment, seeing a pale man and woman come up from the ocean, slowed by sand and tramping toward our fine glass house, I understood I'd built it all for my parents, dead these thirty-odd years, people whose idea of an annual vacation was one spendthrift afternoon at the State Fair outside Raleigh. For a second, in the late light, I thought they'd finally come to collect.

But I was telling you about my career. I cleaned two laundromats for a rich, ill-tempered bachelor. We hardly ever saw each other. He'd leave my pay envelopes in his rural mailbox. He must've liked my work. His will left me both laundromats. I was twenty-five then. I'd been studying law on my own. This first equity helped get me to get a school loan. I made Law Review at Duke. I was thirty-one when I finished.

I moved back here to Falls and bought another laundry unit. I hung up my shingle and started managing the estates of the lawyers and dentists whose widows needed help, whose Princeton sons now practised in flashier cities. The boys had gone off to Atlanta and New York, where real fortunes could be made. I stuck it out locally. In the late fifties, I put new laundromats into the shopping centres that had started opening nearby and all the way into Virginia. Then, with our kids off in good schools, with me spending more time managing my own holdings than other people's, I invented something.

I'd stayed polite and steady, of course, for ever grateful to have a leg up in town society-wise. To this day I follow my dead Mother's advice, I still say 'Please' and 'Thank you very much.' Only now, when I no longer *have* to be polite, only now do people notice my manners and find them humble, touching. Odd. I got somewhat sly. I concocted (with a smart college boy's summer help) and patented (on my own) an adjustable coin-plunger for commercial washers and driers. It used to be the case, when prices went up (as they will), that a laundromat-owner had to rebuy the whole coin-activator component. With my device, the owner can adjust his own machine's templates. He can ask whatever seems fair, and without getting soaked by the manufacturer every time he raises the load-cost by a dime or a quarter. It sounds simple. It is. 'Strictly a nickel and dime operation,' my wife teases me. But I got there first and it has made our financial life a good bit easier.

I took over other laundry facilities. I worked all of it out for my conscience: Washing helps people. My forty-one Carolina/Virginia locations are open to all—all who have some pocket change and the will to stay tidy. Who can argue with the beauty and value of a clean, 100 per cent cotton business shirt, pressed, brand-new, on its hanger and ready-to-wear?

Over my years in business, I have usually been ethical even when it hurt. I'm especially proud of one thing: I volunteered as an unsalaried consultant in a local class-action against the cotton mill here. Nowadays, newspapers call my parents' disease Brown Lung. Thirty years ago we said They've Got What You Get From Working Too Long In The Mill. The Wages of Wages. Clever owners never let anybody *title* the sickness: that meant it wasn't real. The workers won the suit. Japanese-made filters now purify the plant, replacing its entire air supply every twenty minutes. Some new insurance benefits are in place, and there is back pay for those too broken-winded to work.

Though I'm pretty well set now, I've never really felt rich. If that's any defence! My kids have trust funds. Only two bothered finishing college. One teaches the deaf in Savannah. Our middle daughter, Miranda, took Sarah Lawrence by storm and will enter Harvard Law this fall. Our baby girl lives in St Louis with a black airline mechanic who plays jazz on weekends. She says that she's happy. You have to believe them. I know that her living situation shouldn't bother me, but it does.

And I'm not insured. This drives my estate planner crazy. Insurance, based on getting sick, they call Health. The kind depending on everybody's fear of death they call Life! You can have it.

Lately I'll wake up at our beach place and be half out of bed before realizing that I don't have to go to work. It's almost disappointing. I'm finally free. No routes left. I still remember every house along Sunflower Street and Atlantic Avenue, my Eventualities crew.

I have a mind that holds on to the details: the one who told the same three easy riddles, the one in the metal wheelchair who wore a cowgirl hat. A head for facts is good in a lawyer and tinkerer like me. But you can overdo remembering. Recalling too much makes the person inefficient. As I age, early memories become clearer. I still picture many a door opening on those wizened faces, faces probably no older than mine now. I settle back in bed, I listen to the ocean working at reclaiming our ocean-front lot. Having a big, white, glassy house right on the beach should soothe a person. So I lie here looking at the patterns of sunlight-on-water moving across our high, white ceiling. At times, I say—low so as not to wake Millie—'That's over and done.' Then I try to catch more sleep. But you know how it is, once your eyes are open, you can pretend for forty minutes but you're awake for good.

For over thirty-odd years, I've told myself to forget the insurance route. And yet, lately for no good reason, it's been coming back on me, like an over-rich meal.

We all have our crimes. Right?

I remember, after Sam got hold of my list, before he rang up Cleveland with news of impounded funds, that he promised me I'd done the right thing. Sam said I'd fingered fewer Overdues than any collector he could remember, especially for a young collector. They were really ruthless about turning in certain oldsters, these darned eager-beaver kids. Sam claimed I must be good for my clients' morale. 'Thank you,' I said. 'Tried,' I said. Since I'd personally floated many of my old folks' funeral payments for weeks, months—I *was* their morale.

'You're beginning to look better already, Jerry. Know your problem? See, you're like Charlie Chaplin or this Paul Robeson or Mrs Roosevelt maybe—you want to be all things to all people but you can't. Nobody can. Choose maybe four, six, tops. Think of these as job slots you've filled. You get to pick this one handful, then you really better stick your neck out—but just for them. The rest you let go, you've got to, Jerry. Of your six all-time keepers, I seriously doubt one's on this list. Don't say otherwise, Jer. My job? I'm here to make you feel better. You haven't got the Organic Chemistry figured out yet. You're like me—just dripping virtue. There's no percentage in taking it to heart, son. What we're doing here is rigged, sure, but you know why, Jerry? Because it's part of the world.'

As soon as he phoned in our nine worst credit-risks to Cleveland—a town he called 'The Mistake by the Lake'—Sam offered me a drink right from his bottle. This time I took it. My eyes watered. To me the stuff had already started tasting like old couches, the smoky interiors of huts, my Baby Africa route and brown clientele distilled. I drank and drank so I could sleep. My homely boss leaned back, he took his longest, hardest bourbon-pull so far. Dazed, I sat in the office's half-light, drunk. Sam gulped; I kept watching his notched Adam's apple hopping and hopping like a small live thing you pity.

I quit Funerary Eventualities forty years ago. I still feel responsible for the nine who never got the reception they deserve on the next plane. And I don't even *believe* in the next plane. Still, I understand certain basics: Everybody expects a few sure things, a bit of blessed assurance. A person wants to feel covered.

I've kept fretting over this, feeling it for all these years. I mean, basically I'm not all that bad of a man. Am I?

I've never credited any type of heaven. No way. But I still worry for the souls I kept from theirs. Even now I know the names of my nine clients I squealed on. They are:

Betty Seely
Easton Peel
'Junior' Turnage
Carlisle Runyon
Mary Irene Tatum
Leota Saiterwaite
P. M. Hilton
Minna Smith
and Vesta Lotte Battle

I still try and imagine her—on hold, rocking between this world and the next. I want to either bring her back or send her on toward her proper reward. I can't.

Vesta Lotte Battle owed me $12.50.

There, I've told you. I'll feel better. Thank you very much.

GORE VIDAL
EPISTLE TO
THE NEW AGE

Cable News

I have to take a break here in my gospel according to Saint Timothy. Yes, I'm a Saint, after death, of course, which hasn't taken place at this point in time on the present tape. The reason I'm taking a break now is the *Six o'Clock News* is about to go on. I'm afraid I've become addicted to cable-news ever since this complete stranger, Chester W. Claypoole ('Call me Chet'), arrived one day with a television set which he proceeded to rig up in my bungalow just back of the cathedral. I'm Bishop of Macedonia, as you will know in time if you are not lucky enough to be in time already.

On the Road with St Paul

As a Greek boy, I was spotlessly clean. In fact, the second I hit town, any town, I was off to the baths not only for fun and frolic but for oil and pumice-stone, too. Naturally, next to godliness, Saint hated cleanliness—in laypersons, that is. For Saint there was only the One God who had sent his only Son to be crucified and resurrected and then while the rest of us hang around waiting for the end of the world (now slightly overdue according to Saint's original timetable), those who had been associates of our Lord would teach the others how to live in a state of purity—no sex mostly until He comes back and everyone has to appear in court where the good are routed up to Heaven and the rest down to Hell and so on. It's really and truly a wonderful religion, cash-flow-wise, and I say this now from the heart.

Saint worked the circuit like there was no tomorrow, preaching, collecting money, and putting together what was, frankly, the greatest mailing list ever assembled by anyone in the Roman world. Saint had converts everywhere—donors, too. By the time we hit Rome Saint had his own bank—of the Holy Ghost, he used to giggle because, like the Ghost, you had to have faith before you could see where the money was. Saint also invented the numbered account as well as instalment-paying. Although Moses is credited with the invention of double entry book-keeping, Saint developed so many new wrinkles in accounting that the Roman

Internal Revenue service was still trying to untangle them at the time of the fall of same, if that movie with Alec Guinness is to be trusted.

Our first night in Philippi, we visited the old battlefield. There was all the usual tourist-trap stuff except for a meeting of the Brutus Good Name Society in a big hall close to the Ferris wheel. Needless to say, Saint decided then and there to put on a show, using as an excuse his life-long admiration for Brutus, the bastard son of Julius Caesar who helped stab his Dad to death in the theatre of Pompey at Rome where I saw my first Asiatic burlesque show—and I don't mean Asiatic *Minor*. This was Major. *With yellow girls.* A dream. Anyway, a hundred years ago, Brutus was killed in a big battle here by Marc Antony; and they are both now tourist attractions.

Draughty hall. Full of smoke from cheap resin torches. Wooden stage. Statue of Brutus. Maybe a hundred men. Apple-knockers mostly. A few women. Your average Macedonian yokels. Heavy smell. Garlic.

'May I say a few words, Mr Chairperson?' Saint is all simpers and smiles. 'I'm Saul of Tarsus. But also Paul, citizen of Rome.' This always gets a rise in the boondocks where citizens of Rome are pretty thin on the ground. 'I too am an admirer of Brutus, who fell on this very battlefield, a martyr to man's never-ending struggle to preserve slavery.'

The chairperson, a one-eyed rustic, then gives Saint the green light and he's off and running and in no time he is hitting his stride and I unpack the collection plates.

Saint was not tall, contrary to legend. He was maybe five feet at the most, like Jesus, but where Jesus was enormously fat with this serious hormonal problem—the so-called parable about the loaves and fishes was just the fantasy of somebody who could never get enough to eat—Paul's body was thin and carpeted with short black hairs like a spider except for the big head which was bald. All he had going for him, was this beautiful speaking voice like the *Sunday Hour of Power and Prayer* man my wife's so taken with. And of course how Saint could lie! I've never known anyone who could make things up so quickly and so plausibly when he was really wired, and wired he was that night in Philippi, preaching to all those Brutus fans.

After a series of truly inspired improvised anecdotes about Brutus, stories never heard before or since because Saint had never had the occasion to make them up before, he segues smoothly into his Road to Damascus routine and I will say this: as often as I heard this particular rap—ten thousand times? I never got tired of it. There was something God-given as we Greeks say—charismatic to you—in Saint's delivery. Also the Yellow Brick Road story was never the same twice. I used to think that Saint's creative changes would be confusing to our flaks—particularly Mark who has to keep feeding his processor with the 'true' Jesus story in competition with Saint's recollections of Jesus, whom he never met except as a sort of ghost on the road to Damascus, but Mark says that the different versions are actually very helpful to him as he puts together the True Story of the Good News that Jesus brought all the world about the end of the world, to be later added to by Saint ('Call me Sol') Paul in his correspondence to yours truly, Timothy, among others. But Mark—or Saint Mark as he'll be promoted to unless the TV people are giving me the run-around, says that Saint's stories don't have to make sense because he, Mark, is redoing the whole story anyway. I wonder if Chet has got in touch with Mark, who is still alive I'm told, not that that makes any difference if we're all on tapes and Chet can just do a fast rewind to where Mark is alive and writing his Gospel. What, I wonder, does Chet really want?

It's interesting how everyone connected with this circus has his own axe to grind which is why, I suppose, I'm grinding mine right now. For instance, I think that suppressing Jesus's weight problem gives us a distorted view of his psychology which was itself distorted—if not pretty peculiar. There are also other aspects of His mission to the soon-to-be late great planet earth that have been completely omitted by Mark and the others, not to mention the key fact which is becoming more and more obvious—Jesus isn't coming back any time soon, and if there is to be a Judgement Day, it's going to happen way in the future, on cable television probably—at least that's my hunch.

Saint's Philippi version of how he was converted to Christianity (which he hadn't yet invented!) was particularly vivid as he described seeing the ghost of our founder on the east-bound Jerusalem-Damascus freeway. 'I had been a persecutor, my friends.

Yea! Of Brutus. Nay! I mean Jesus. But then is not each the same in that he was persecuted for his goodness by a vile humanity?' Saint could make even a slip of the tongue become like a clashing cymbal. 'I had been hired by Mossad, the dreaded secret service apparatus of the Roman Palestinian-Zionist Lobby. I had been ordered to spy on all those who wished to make their peace with God who had sent them his only Son—the only Daughter is for later, for Judgement Day—to show mankind the road to Heaven. So there I was. A hot day. Palm trees. A mirage shivering in the middle distance. A camel. A pyramid. Your average Middle Eastern landscape as viewed from the freeway. Complete with burning bush. Suddenly. HE. WAS. THERE.'

In that silent smoky hall you could have heard a pin drop or the loosest foreskin slide back. 'Wide as he was tall, Jesus waddled toward me.' To live audiences, Saint often let this sort of detail slip out. But in his writing, never. 'That face. Those luminous eyes hidden somewhere in all that golden fat. The ineffable smile like the first slice from a honeydew melon. Oh, delight! He held up a hand, a tiny starfish cunningly fashioned of lard. He spoke, his voice so high, so shrill that only the odd canine ever got the whole message, hence the need for interpretation and self-consciousness—in short, mega-fiction.' Saint could make even literary theory sing when he wanted to and he wanted to that night at Philippi. '"Why," shrilled the Son of the One God, "dost thou persecuteth me-th?"' Saint always went ye-olde whenever he quoted Our Saviour. But saviour from *what*? This has never occurred to me before, and I'm a bishop. Sin, I suppose. But we've all given up on that, if the truth were known. Certainly Jesus wasn't going to save us *from* Judgement Day or from Hell either since he's part of the Whole Judicial Process, I suppose he intends to get his friends and fund-raisers off. I must give some real thought to this little loose end of our generally well-knit by now doctrine of Christianity.

Anyway, the folks ate up the ye-olde stuff. They also liked the fact that our Saviour, at least according to Saint, never said anything that your Aunt Minerva wouldn't have said after a long day of in-depth shopping so they always liked it when Saint dressed up the act a bit, by throwing in miracles and recipes and grooming hints galore.

Folks really like miracles and this is the age of them, too. Real ones, I mean. Like television. Naturally, we've been known to rig a miracle or two. Like raising from the dead someone who's actually alive but painted green and so on. But there is simply no way of explaining Chet's visit to me, and all the other strange people who've been monitoring us.

When I used to discuss these creepy visitors with Saint, he'd clam up. I bring up the subject now because the first one I ever saw—*knew* that I saw, that is—was that night at Philippi. I now know that Saint had more dealings with them than he ever let on: 'Angels in disguise,' he'd mutter. My own current hunch is that those peculiar visitors back then—now, too—were—and are—on the prowl for commercial franchises to our product, which means getting in on the ground floor of this definitely up-market growth-oriented religion we've been inventing which is firmly based on the absolutely true word of the One God in his three sections, each suitable for worship taken in part or as a whole and guaranteed to dress up any residence or soul tastefully.

Saint played that Macedonian audience like a twelve-string lute in the hands of a love-mad Lesbian Islander. 'The hand, the *hand*! That was the proof. Because in the centre of each palm there was this hole where He had been tacked to the cross by a nail. I knew then that it was HIM—HE.' Saint always adjusted his grammar to the audience and never the audience to the grammar. But then we saints are born knowing all the tricks of the trade, including the halo. Even so, Saint had one trick that nobody else has ever mastered. When you go into all that genealogy of how J.C. is descended from King David and so on the result is not only boring but absolutely mystifying for a civilian audience that doesn't know the difference between a Jew and a Chinaman. So how did Saint get through the dull parts? He invented, all by himself, *with no professional guidance of any kind*, tap-dancing.

Saint had these copper cleats attached to the soles of his sandals. When he started with the 'begats', he would start dancing, back and forth across the stage, the taps preceding and succeeding each 'begat' and then, grand finale, a tap between the 'be' and the 'gat' until by the time he gets past the begats Abendigo to HIM, he was like a simian bow-legged Astaire who my wife adores on the

TV. Personally, I wouldn't put Saint in Astaire's class but he was certainly every bit as good as Dan Dailey, which is high praise.

Well, Saint had those Macedonian yokels clapping their hands and tapping their toes as he gave out with the message, Hallelujah! 'The form of this world is a'changin. It's all a'gonna end real soon. Them's who worship false gods, are in for eternal torment. But us'n'll be saved. And that's a promise. *If*'n you follow Him. 'Cause with Him—He—Hi-Ho! the law of Moses got itself crossed-out. Crossed-out! That's the *Good* News, folks!'

Usually Saint didn't do Moses-bashing with the goyim on the ground that they wouldn't know what he was talking about. But once he was launched on one of his raps, you never knew what was going to come out. Anyway, that hot muggy day night in Philippi, by the time he came to the 'And now a pair of young brothers in the Lord will pass among you with their collection plates and some literature which is absolutely *gratis* for an obel' ending, I knew that we had started up yet another church because that's how we did it back then. First a hell-fire sermon from Saint. Then the collection. Then names and addresses for our master Rolodex. Then Saint would take appointments for baptisms and so on. Finally, before skipping town, he'd appoint some deacons and deaconesses and lo! and behold the First Pauline Church of Philippi would open its doors for business.

Angels in Disguise

As Silas and I made our way through that revved-up crowd, accepting donations with the far-away smile Saint had taught us, I noticed a strange little woman, wearing a black costume that I did not recognize at the time. Since Chet's arrival at my bungalow with the television, I've since learned a lot about the different costumes in the TV part of the world. But in those days everybody just wore his tunic and maybe his cloak or toga on top of that and that was about it for the guys. The gals wore these wrap-arounds.

The lady in the black non-wrap-around was my very first 'angel in disguise'.

She was watching us with an expression that was pretty much beyond rapt. She had, I realize now, just channelled in from the TV world. At this point in Saint's history, he had been in touch with these visitors for some time, although he preferred not to talk about them to us. One of the few times he ever opened up on the subject was when we were in Rome and I was shacked up with a rich widow called Flavia on the Aventine. Saint was in a state of deep depression over a lot of things, including the widow and my having told him that my hyacinthine golden curls and blue forget-me-not eyes were now strictly out of bounds as far as he was concerned, ass-wise.

We were at breakfast. In a loggia. View of cemetery across Tiber. View of Tiber. Lot of barges from Ostia. Stacked with amphorae. Sun like a round hot . . . thing. In the sky. *Blue* sky. Blue—Saint started in on how blue he was and how unhappy his life had been and how, worst of all, he was a phoney because he'd never bothered to meet Jesus before he died. 'There I was in Tarsus. Practically next door to Jerusalem. Go see Jesus? You kidding? No time. Sorry. Too busy. Well, I *was* busy putting out a line of ready-made tents but what really kept my nose to the grindstone was my under-cover work for Mossad. Yes, darling, I was an agent of the dreaded secret service of the Roman Palestinian-Zionist Lobby. I was one of their numerous hit-men, Call me Sol. My code name. I set up Stephen to be hit. And, baby, he was hit. Just like we got Count Bernadotte. Pow! I also had orders to keep an eye on subversive self-hating Jews like Jesus. But did I? No. Too boring, I thought. Too many losers to check out. Then *He* meets me on the freeway after He died. Oh, I could kick myself. Just about everybody and his brother in Greater Israel had heard Him, seen Him. You know, Timmy, it is my personal educated guess that, so far, to date, in this frame of time, more than one million have personally checked Him out and that's just a fraction of all those *outside* the frame who'll keep on coming and coming, wanting tickets, cost no object, for the crucifixion scene at Golgotha, the grand finale, in every version—and *I* wasn't there, ever. To date, that is.'

My head was spinning. 'A million *who* were where? Not people. There aren't that many people in Greater Jerusalem even if you count the Arabs.'

Saint realized that he had blundered. He batted his eyelids at me, an old trick when he was about to lie or change the subject. But I didn't let up. So finally he said, 'Well, I meant . . . you know, the kibbitzers. The monitors like the one we saw that night at Philippi. Remember her?'

So sitting there in the loggia of Flavia's attractive if somewhat bitter better home and garden on the Aventine Hill, I suddenly remembered what had happened back then, which I now record.

Saint, Silas and I were at the back of the hall behind the stage with no one around and only a couple of smoky torches for light. Silas and I were busy counting the money while Saint was copying out names to put in the Rolodex.

Suddenly, like out of nowhere, the strange little woman reappears. She clutches at Saint's arm. 'I saw you at Lystra.' She had no accent at all, to my ear anyway. Yet she was certainly not Greek. 'I saw you heal the man with the crippled foot.'

'I know.' Saint was very calm. 'I saw you, too. Sit down, Madam. Timmy, give her your seat.'

'I'll stand.' She stared at Saint, eyes like inflamed egg yolks. 'Wherever you heal with faith, there I am. Or try to be. It isn't always easy to get through.'

'Where there's a will there's a way—as He said.' Saint's lack of curiosity about who she was—not to mention from where—should have clued me in that he was on to what I came to think of as the phantom phoney folks. After Philippi, there were a lot of them, particularly on important occasions. Odd. I haven't seen one for years now except for Chet. No, that isn't quite true.

Last month, I met one who was doing a study of Saint's correspondence. He tracked me down in the New Star Baths across from the proconsul's palace. He was very nervous and wore what I now know from the television were glasses and a hearing-aid. 'I can't believe it,' he kept saying. We were in the tepidarium, never crowded at that hour. He was holding a folder in one hand. 'What have you got there?' I asked.

'New versions of Saint Paul's letters to Timothy. You . . . you . . . you must be Timothy.' Like a shepherd the man was aquake with awe while his hearing-aid buzzed at me like a locust announcing a plague of same.

I took the letters from him. They had been typed up in Greek like the newspapers you see on television. I recognized some of our correspondence, with all of Saint's complaining and advising. Then I came across a very peculiar letter where Saint recalls his activities with Mossad and some of the early anti-Christian plots that he had been a part of, including arson at a certain well-known hostelry in downtown Jerusalem. 'He never wrote me about this,' I said. 'And besides, that was long before he saw the Light.'

'Are you sure, Saint Timothy?' The man gave me the chills, even in the tepidarium.

'I should know what he wrote me even when sometimes he didn't bother to mail it but had it copied and spread around the churches.'

'But our computer analysis, always correct, with a four per cent margin of error, clearly shows that this was written by Saint Paul . . .'

Then the man was gone as quickly as he had arrived from nowhere. He will be back. I'm sure of that. Why?

Now—back to Philippi and the little lady in black who said, 'Do you not agree with me, Saint Paul, that illness is simply a manifestation of a weakening of mind?'

'All things are contained within the single-mind of the One True God in his three aspects.' Saint could dispense this sort of absolutely seamless theology while taking apart and reassembling a complex Rolodex machine, which is exactly what he was doing. He was a lousy tent-maker but when it came to any office equipment that involved paying customers, he had digital dexterity in spades.

'I study you every chance I get,' she said. 'Which is not as often as I'd like because I must make myself ill first, which goes against my whole nature, a perversion really, of mind itself. But I have no choice. That is why I deliberately fill up on Welsh rarebit, which I detest. Then I sleep and dream, horrid dreams of olden times filled with hideous people and ghastly smells,' she was staring with revulsion at Saint's tunic. Time to burn it, I duly noted. 'Then suddenly I am in the Holy Land, where I behold you in the act of healing through Right Thinking, and it is worth the rumbling bowels, the acid indigestion, the horrendous hangover next day because, in addition to Welsh rarebit, let me confess that I imbibe gin neat or even, sometimes, as now, a gin daisy, a tasty cocktail if one were not, as I am, temperance.'

'So, drunk out of your skull, Madam, you are transported to me, here in the olden, golden times. I am flattered. What is a gin daisy?'

'Three parts gin to one part Cointreau, and a maraschino cherry. Oh, it is vile.'

I realize now that this was my first *significant* encounter with one of the kibbitzers, as Saint called them. When I asked him why they should want to . . . to kibbitz, he would change the subject. He did warn me not to take anything they said seriously. This was easy since during our travels we must have met every freak in the world and they were all a kind of blur to us. Besides, who listened? After all, we were, to be blunt, in show business and there was a lot of classy competition in those days, particularly when it came to miracles, the heaviest part of anybody's act.

The lady in black had seen our Lord only the one time when he raised Lazarus from the dead. 'Oh, I had to be there for that caper. Because it proved my point perfectly. You see, Lazarus was not dead *because there is no death*. As death is bad and God is good, and if God is everything and everything is God, then death cannot exist.' Well, I've heard dumber arguments, and in our own church, too.

'Madam, Lazarus was dead as a mackerel.' Saint was smooth, fingers busy with the Rolodex.

'No. He may have looked to you like the proverbial mackerel but that was only his appearance. There is the *appearance* of death as there is the appearance of evil but these appearances are *inside* the viewer when he has been thinking wrong thoughts, negative thoughts, though they don't exist *outside*, where God . . . '

'Three parts of gin to one of vermouth?'

'Cointreau. I'm getting a headache now, and I'll soon be taking the channel-boat home. So I must be quick. I had no time at Lystra to ask you if you don't agree that it's *all* in the mind? Bad living, bad thoughts, death, illness . . . '

'Mind is God. God is mind, of course, dear lady, of course. But to be mackerel-defunct is the exact opposite of being merry-grig funct and so . . . '

The lady clapped her hands, eyes aswim with tears. 'You agree! I knew you would. I've based so much of my work in the lab on this higher knowledge that I am eager for your scientific validation. You see, I am, through God, a scientific healer not of souls but of minds. I am, I like to think, as strictly scientific in my approach as He was that day with the mackerel named Lazarus. Because, dangerously overweight or not . . . '

'Lazarus.'

'Jesus. Our Lord. Such a pity. The first of all doctors and healers cannot heal himself. Fat as a butter ball. Bad colour. Short of breath. Naturally, he was obliged to live as a human being. But why gorge on codfish cakes? Scrod? Boiled beef, baked beans, Indian pudding?'

'Dishes not native to Palestine, I fear . . . '

'Scrapple. Whatever . . . '

'Halvah was a weakness of our Lord. A kilo of mashed beans with olive oil was also a favourite—usually as a pre-sermon snack. Give him the carbohydrates and he'd let the proteins go. Naturally, he was a martyr to flatulence. Even after he was dead when we met on the . . . '

'I know the story.' She cut Saint short. 'There is no death. It is all in the mind.' She gave a loud belch; turned pink with embarrassment. 'Oh, dear. Forgive me. The Welsh rarebit is repeating.'

'I had not finished,' said Saint mildly. 'Let me tell you His own words to me on the freeway. Although a ghost, he looked just as he did in life except for a certain tendency to let the light shine through him. "How," he asked me, "can I, at this weight, be a convincing Holy Ghost?" Well, I took the bull by the horns and said, "Look, there's been talk of splitting you up into three parts—dad, son, ghost. Now if you were to be in the three sections . . . "'

The lady gave a terrible cry. 'I hate this! I'm nauseated. Presently I shall be nauseous as well. Three parts . . . '

'Of gin to one of Cointreau. You've told me twice now. Anyway, *I* told Jesus, straight from the shoulder, that although this new doctrine was only on the drawing-board, for his own peace of mind he could still go off to Gaza to this fat-farm, run by an old pal of mine from Mossad, Ben Hur. You remember him? How he beat the Roman in the chariot race by cheating? Well, he's now in the fat-farm business and, get this! health food, too. Ben swears that a gramme of marinated locusts and dried goat-dung a day . . . .'

The lady gave an eldritch scream. 'My card,' she added, opening her reticule and withdrawing a calling card which Saint took just as she vanished with the mournful words, 'Oh, my head!'

'I'll bet she has a hangover to end all hangovers. Cointreau with gin is a killer.'

'What's her name?' Silas was moderately interested.

'Mary Baker Eddy,' Saint read from the card. 'She's pastor of the Church of Christ, Scientist, in Boston, wherever that is.'

'Spain,' said Silas who had travelled quite a lot. 'Is this the same Christ as ours?'

'I doubt it. But I do think we're in for a lot of copyright infringements'.

Automatically Paul put her name on the Rolodex. As he used to say, you never know who's got the money. 'It's tough trying to hang on to a trademark. James-brother-of-our-Lord even went so far as to hire this smart Jew lawyer in Rome who specializes in copyright cases but, so far, all he's been able to do is collect a large fee every quarter. James-brother-of-our-Lord is a schmuck because the problem is not how do you copyright the word Christ, which you can't, but the cross as logo, which you can. Of course *Pauline* Christianity might be easier to copyright but,' Saint whinnied happily, 'that would be sacrilege, wouldn't it?'

Silas and I then jumped him, tore off his tunic, and burned it by the Ferris wheel. Then we dumped the howling Saint into a nearby river.

Thus it was that we established the church at Philippi, in the presence of Mary Baker Eddy of Boston, Spain.

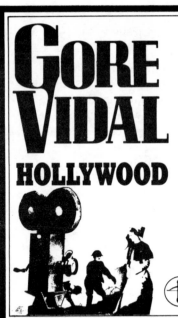

MARTHA GELLHORN
THE INVASION
OF PANAMA

Panamanian President Guillermo Endara (right) with American troops.

W e drove too fast on a dark road; there was no other traffic. Everything had been going too fast from the moment of arrival at Panama's airport. A bent bony little man seized my luggage and ran with it, shouting, 'Hurry, *Señora*, I have no salary, I live on tips!' Immigration and customs were only a pause. The porter dumped my stuff on the pavement. A taxi driver shouted, 'Come, *Señora*, with three it costs only eight dollars to the centre!' I was hustled into his car where two passengers waited. I thought all this rush and noise were hysterical. What was the matter with these people?

The young Costa Rican sitting next to me said he was going by bus tomorrow to buy merchandise in the Free Zone at Colón, at the Caribbean end of the Canal, and if God wills would be back in Costa Rica the next day.

The middle-aged Panamanian in the front seat said, 'Noriega used to run the Free Zone. Now it's a nephew of Endara.' They all laughed. Endara is the new President of Panama, installed by the US Invasion.

Then the panic talk started. I heard a variation of it every day from everyone I met.

'This is a very dangerous place,' said the Costa Rican. 'I do not like to come here. There are robbers everywhere. They have weapons. If you do not give them what they want, they kill you. You should not be travelling alone.'

The Panamanian passenger said, 'Never be out after nine o'clock.' It was now nearly half-past nine. 'Do not walk on the streets alone. If you take money, take only what you need and hold your purse close to your side.'

The taxi driver asked: 'Which is your hotel?'

I said any hotel in the centre would do.

They discussed this and the driver said, 'I will take you to the Ejecutivo; it is clean and comfortable and safe.' *Seguro* was the operative word.

We turned off the wide street by a lighted petrol station. High board fences lined both sides of a narrow street. 'Those stores were looted,' said the front-seat passenger. 'Everyone stole—not only the poor, the rich too.' We stopped in the dark and waited until the Panamanian had opened his front door and gone inside. They dropped me at the Ejecutivo with renewed serious warnings to take much care.

At ten o'clock, I stood on the first-floor balcony of my very clean, very comfortable, safe room and looked at a dead city. No movement, no sound, no lights. The curfew was at midnight. Panama had been famous for its nightlife, a wide-open town. This was almost three months after the Invasion.

I had to change traveller's cheques, and my delightful hotel nestled among banks and closed night clubs. The banks have a Pharaoh complex; there are 140 of them. They are towers or palaces, monuments to money. A mirrored skyscraper, with SWISS BANK in red neon on top, gleamed nearby. Why not be brave and walk? The streets in this part of town were wide and clean, every building opulent, white, with decorative planting. No one was walking.

When I reached the air-conditioned bank foyer I was drenched in sweat, a sensible reason for not walking. To my surprise the Swiss Bank used only a few floors in the middle of the tower. To my greater surprise I found myself in a small, linoleum-floored hall, with a wood shelf and a man behind a dirty glass teller's window. No, they didn't do retail business; this was an international bank, engaged in shipping money around the world. He said that the Invasion had closed the commercial banks for a few days. But 24,000 armed men, attack helicopters, tanks and riotous disorder in the city had not interfered for an hour with international banking.

The commercial bank, very grand, had an armed private guard in front of its locked, iron grille door. The teller gave me a wad of used dollar bills. Money in Panama is American. Due to two years of the US embargo, supplies of new dollar bills ceased. Paper which has changed hands for all this time is so worn and foul that it feels like oncoming skin disease. Now, stiff with cash, I hailed a taxi though the bank was only a few long, hot blocks from my hotel. The taxis are little beat-up cars, like fast water beetles, with room for three passengers; they collect trade as they go. The fare is a dollar for any distance. You flag one down and if it is headed in your direction, you hop in with the others. This taxi driver said, 'Be very careful. Many taxi drivers have been robbed and killed. It is worse than war here.'

I put my fortune in the hotel safe and set out to improve my looks. There was a beauty salon on the side street by the hotel. While her assistant washed my hair, the jolly, blowsy hairdresser said, 'People stole anything, from viciousness not need. Twenty-five beauty salons were robbed of everything, even the wash-basins. Noriega stole and he taught the people to steal. There was such corruption here; it was a sickness. They left this street alone except for the jewellery shop. Where I live was not harmed. Only the houses of the poor were destroyed.'

I was slow to understand the catastrophe of looting that ravaged the whole of Panama City for three days, beginning the day after the US night invasion on 20 December. The structure of the state was wiped out in the six hours of the main attack. US Southern Command, the permanent military establishment in Panama, had created a vacuum in civil order, but did not recognize that it was obligated to patrol and protect the city. The troops had no orders to do so. The people turned into mad locusts, swarming through the streets. At the time it must have seemed like the biggest wildest happiest drunken binge ever known, courtesy of the US Army. The hangover is painful; Panama has not yet recovered. 'I saw American soldiers sitting in a tank, watching,' said the hairdresser.

I asked about the US embargo, which starved Nicaragua and has been a crippling burden on Cuba for thirty years. In Panama, it was meant to cause hardship and popular discontent that would drive out Noriega. She shrugged. 'There was always plenty to eat in Panama. We lacked for nothing.' In fact, the embargo reduced Panama's gross national product by twenty per cent, but hurt mainly the rich, the white business community, since the United States is Panama's major trading partner.

As I needed to buy a plane ticket and there was a travel agency a few doors away, I took my problem to a stylishly dressed, thirty-something business woman, who reserved a ticket quickly on her computer. She said, 'The United States created that monster; they knew Noriega well. They even *decorated* him. He has been in power here for twenty-one years.'

I asked what it was like to live here in those years.

'Nothing happened to people like me under Noriega. If you were neutral it was all right. Mostly the poor favoured Noriega.'

Her facts were not entirely correct. Panama had indeed been a military dictatorship for twenty-one years, which did not disturb the US government until two years ago. Noriega was the intelligence chief of General Torrijos, the previous military overlord. Noriega had been top man for six years, behind a president and legislature and elections, the way the United States likes things to look. But it is correct that American governments knew Noriega well during three decades. Noriega did not suddenly become a drug-dealing fiend in the last two years, after a blameless life. President Carter took him off the CIA payroll; President Reagan put him back.

I asked about the banks: why build those immense, unneeded towers?

'They rented out their extra space for offices,' she said. 'There will be many empty offices now. You know this city was called "the washing machine". Anybody could open an office and be a banker and launder money, no questions asked.' The cowboy bankers may be gone but the useful secrecy laws remain.

The heat was heavy, a weight on your body, and the sun was blinding. I said I must buy sun-glasses and shirts; I would be changing them four times a day. 'Shop around here, on Via España. Do not go downtown. Above all don't go near Central. They will see you're a foreigner: you will be robbed immediately.' Central is the main popular shopping street in Chorrillo, the district that took the worst blast of the Invasion.

There were three giant round-ups while I was in Panama. Before dawn, 500 to 700 American soldiers and the new Panamanian paramilitary police blocked off poor sections of the city with tanks and made house-to-house searches. The first, most publicized round-up netted 726 'anti-socials', largely illegal Colombian immigrants, forty-six revolvers and a minor supply of drugs, average for private use. The triumphant catch was a tall, skinny twenty-year-old black, nicknamed Half Moon, a gang leader 'accused of four assassinations'. The papers carried no further mention of anti-socials in later round-ups and no reports of mugging, armed robbery, not even pickpockets. It was finally admitted that there was no great hidden arms cache in the city, nor any sizeable quantity of drugs. Without reason, the people are certain that Panama is overrun by cut-throat criminals, and the panic talk never stops. I think this pervasive fear was shell-shock from the terror of the Invasion, something like an unconscious mass nervous breakdown.

208

The traffic of the capital city, which is called simply Panama, hurtles at race-track speed along the streets. There are no traffic-lights. They were knocked out two years ago in a general strike, to disrupt the city. They were not replaced but Noriega had tough traffic cops, armed with .45s, and drivers dreaded fines or prison sentences. In my first days there were no traffic cops. Then a few began to appear with day-glo gloves and vests. These uncertain men, all blacks, belong to the new Panamanian paramilitary police. US Southern Command vetted Noriega's former soldiers on a scale ranging from black (downright bad) to grey (neutral) to white (harmless). It selected a chosen number and gave them a new name. They are no longer the Defence Force; they are the Public Force and their barracks now bear the words Policia Nacional. They have also been given a new humiliating uniform, a loose, belted khaki shirt, baggy khaki trousers and floppy khaki hat, like a sun-hat.

The people, who find this laughable, are told that this force with new commanders and new orders to be polite and helpful, are new men. But wherever authority must be imposing, there are six-foot-tall, white American soldiers, with M-16 rifles, and those somehow ominous boots and camouflage uniforms, and nobody doubts for a minute who is in charge here: US Southern Command.

My watch-strap broke; I went in search of a watch shop. Advised and directed by people on the street, I found a hole-in-the-wall store, looted clean of its stock, including watch-straps. This small businessman was bankrupt. Insurance, if he had any, does not cover acts of war. The city-wide vandalism was the sequel to an act of war. A slim, neatly dressed young man, chatting with the unemployed proprietor, offered to take me to Central on a bus to buy a strap.

The buses, like the taxis, belong to their drivers and are a treat. They have girls' names and fanciful decorations painted on their sides: a puffing steam locomotive, a sylvan scene, a luscious blonde on the rear end. When you want to get off you shout '*parada*', stop, pay fifteen cents and jump down. Juan, my new friend, and I got off at the lower end of Via España, a street more or less comparable to Regent Street. Opposite was the Archaeological Museum and a big Chase Manhattan Bank, both looted. Juan felt awful about the

Photo: James Nachtwey (Magnum)

museum. 'It is our history,' he said. 'Now it is gone.'

Central begins here and it looked a mess, litter, garbage, but it is a genuine Panamanian street that still has the charm of liveliness. Every building had been looted and, though some had re-opened and some like McDonald's were operating behind boards instead of window-glass, many remained empty and ruined. The effect was of a recently bombed city. Juan pointed to an untouched shop, offering Oriental wares. 'The owners are Pakistanis; they protected their place with guns.' We found a watch-strap.

Juan insisted on taking me to his flat in Chorrillo. We walked down narrow slum streets, stepping around garbage. The houses here were big, old, unpainted wood boxes, four storeys high, filthy, packed with people, the balconies draped in drying laundry. I heard that these structures were built in the early years of the century as boarding houses for the men who dug the Canal. Chorrillo is the poorest and most densely populated district of a long strung-out city where 600,000 people live. At this end, the poverty is stunning; at the other end, wealth is flaunted.

Juan, an accountant, lives on the twelfth floor of a tower-block, one of several rising above the ancient grey wood warrens. The entry was dark and miserable, but once out on the open walkway that led to the flats, you saw how proudly these people took care of their homes. Juan's spotless, cramped flat was blissfully cool, wind blowing through from the back door to the front balcony. It has beautiful views: behind to green Ancon Hill, HQ for Southern Command; in front to the Pacific and the beginning of the Canal. Juan shares the meagre space with his wife and three infant sons, the fourth well on the way. Here his family, and everyone else in the building, was wakened shortly after midnight on 20 December by the inconceivable noise of bombardment.

'We all ran to the basement,' Juan said. 'We lay on the floor for six hours. We were terrified. The children have traumas.' (Trauma, misused, has now entered the Spanish language in Panama.) When the noise died down they went back to their flats. A machine-gun bullet slashed across one wall of Juan's balcony; the windows were broken. For three days this area was without electricity, for five days without water.

Almost opposite Juan's building, three streets away, Noriega had established his main Cuartel, a compound of headquarters and barracks, set in the midst of the slums. Perhaps Noriega felt most comfortable here because this is what he came from, an illegitimate abandoned slum kid. That Cuartel was the focus for the US Invasion. Noriega was not there and never had been. But the poor were sleeping in their overcrowded tenements all around, and there they died, unless they managed to escape. Juan took photos from his balcony right after the attack. It looked the way any city looks, subjected to modern warfare; like a wilderness of jagged teeth. Juan was most impressed by his photos of crumpled burned private cars.

'What did that?' he asked.

'I'd guess machine-gun fire from helicopters.'

'Do you see the bodies inside?'

American army engineers bulldozed the area, as much as they could, and now it is a grey stony wasteland, about six city blocks in size. Apparently to shift the blame for the death and destruction in Chorrillo, the story was put about that it was the work of Noriega's Dignity Brigade, his special thug bodyguard. While pinned down in the Cuartel by helicopter gunships, rockets, tanks and US infantry, men of the Dignity Brigade are supposed to have crept out and set fire to the surrounding slums.

The magazine *Army*, in its account of Operation Just Cause, prints a photo of a sky-high black cloud which it describes as a fire in a Cuartel building, 'the result of heavy damage inflicted by air support and Sheridan light tanks.' The Cuartel buildings were cement and would not have burned like that, but the dry old wood tenements burned to the ground. Again as reported by *Army*, some of Noriega's troops escaped from the Cuartel and sniped at American soldiers from the upper floors of the tenements. Since when are snipers silenced by erasing whole city blocks crammed with civilians?

After the Invasion, we read in our newspapers first that there were 300, then later 600 dead in Panama. The consensus on the streets of Panama is 7,000 dead. Chorrillo was a death-trap. There was also heavy fighting in San Miguelito, north-east of the airport where another Noriega Cuartel is encircled by slums. 'You cannot see that,' I was told. 'They have their Cuartel there now.' 'They' are always Americans. 'It is closed off by barbed wire. But you could smell the dead, a horrible smell, two days later.' Juan also spoke of

smelling the dead in Chorrillo, three days after the invasion. It is a smell you know at once though you never knew it before; and you never forget it.

You are not allowed to see San Miguelito, but any taxi driver will take you to the Garden of Peace, a large, private cemetery near there. The cemetery is an expanse of perfectly tended lawn with identical small, flat marble gravestones. A trench of chocolate-coloured earth runs across the rear width of the cemetery. A mass grave. This mass grave is common knowledge. Rumour says there is another mass grave at Fort Amador, now occupied by US Southern Command. Rumour says that there are several more.

In early January, a group of well-known Americans—lawyers, clergy, civil rights activists, students, trade union leaders—formed the Independent Commission of Inquiry on the US Invasion of Panama. Ramsey Clark, former US attorney general, the Commission's principal spokesman, made several trips to Panama. On 25 January, the Commission sent out a press release: 'Having spoken to hospital personnel, cemetery and morgue workers and others with first-hand accounts, we believe that as many as 4,000 to 7,000 people may have been killed during the Invasion.' No one knows the number of the wounded—hundreds? thousands?—and they are unseen. The Panamanian authorities admit that 15,000 families were made homeless, in one night.

I went out to dinner once, hoping for a good meal, but it was too spooky, only five other people in the restaurant and nerves about finding a taxi to get back to the hotel by nine o'clock. The empty streets suggested that everyone had nine o'clock nerves. At night I read the Panama papers. The news was mostly bland waffle. Every day, the 'fast' of President Endara made the front pages. In these chaotic times, the President had withdrawn to the Cathedral, where he 'fasted', 'out of compassion for the humble people who are suffering hunger' and to gain 'a more spiritual outlook'.

The humble people jeered. They said that the President was a fat man of fifty-three dieting to lose weight for his June wedding to Ana Mae, aged twenty-four. In a brilliantly lit side chapel, whose altar was adorned with a truly hideous plaster statue of the dead

Christ in Mary's arms and big vases of artificial flowers, President Endara received diplomats and delegations and starved on mustard-coloured varnished wood pews. He slept there on a cot. The Presidential piety was much appreciated by the Church. The President fasted for thirteen days, lost seventeen pounds and returned to his offices in the Presidential palace, a handsome white building that faces the sea. Here a small group of protesters, bearing hand-printed placards, camps silently on the cobbles across from the guarded entrance. One placard stated: 'No one talks of fasting who knows hunger.' Another announced: 'Noriega robbed us, Endara locks us up.'

Everyone asks where you come from. I said *Inglaterra* which is true. Now I intended to present myself as a *'periodista inglesa'*, an English journalist, at the *Casa de Periodistas*, the modest compound of meeting rooms, courtyard, tatty bar and union offices of Panamanian journalists. I wanted people to talk to me, and I refused to take any responsibility for the Invasion.

The *Casa de Periodistas* buzzed with arguing, sloppily dressed men; journalism cannot be a road to riches here. The first protest demo, called by the National Council of Workers' Organizations, was due that afternoon outside Parliament. I had been gripped by the human misery and the wreckage of the Invasion; I had no idea of its political effect until I met the press.

Upstairs in the union office, a man said: 'American troops went to people's homes; they arrested all union officials within three days. They took them to Clayton [Fort Clayton, the main US Southern Command base] for interrogation. They took our pictures. I was held for three days. Some colleagues for weeks, some we still don't know about. US soldiers moved in here and occupied the place. They only gave it back on 18 January [nearly a month after the Invasion]. About 150 journalists in the private and public sector have been sacked. *Not* Noriegistans, by God, but anti-gringo. I expect to be picked up any day.'

'There are American advisors in every department of the government, telling Endara's people what to do,' another journalist said. 'It is against the Panamanian Constitution to have foreigners in our government.'

An angry man said: 'They sacked 2,000 civil servants, including

217

all the union officials, without any kind of legality. There are 30,000 more unemployed since the Invasion. The worst is that the real hacks, people who took part in the corruption of the Noriega regime, are now part of this new government and saying who should be fired, protecting their own people. If you are against the Invasion, they say you are Noriegista. Soon they will say we are communists. We are *nationalists*.'

This journalist spoke with bitterness. '*Radio Nacional* stayed on the air after the Invasion, telling people what was happening. A day later, a helicopter circled their building three times until it got into position, then it fired a rocket into the seventh floor. That took care of *Radio Nacional*. Then they arrested its director Ruben Dario. The newspaper *La Republica* came out with reports of the dead, after the Invasion. The next day American soldiers went in and smashed up the offices and closed the paper. They kept Calvo, the editor, in Fort Clayton for about six weeks; now he's in the Model Prison. We haven't heard of any charge against him. Southern Command closed two other newspapers and they've taken over TV channels 2 and 4 [Panama channels]. To move freely in our own country we need a press card from Southern Command. We haven't the right to know how many people died because General Cisneros [of Southern Command] took the list. Information is the property of Southern Command, not the Panamanian press. This isn't a democracy; it's a US military dictatorship, instead of a Noriega dictatorship.'

'Noriega is nothing, an excuse,' an older journalist said. 'They can't even bring him to trial. First they said March; now they say January 1991. They'll hide him away and in five years he'll be free to enjoy his millions. This Invasion is about the Canal Treaty. The United States has put in a docile government, the oligarchy, the same class we had in 1968. It has the same interests as the United States. There must be an election in 1994, according to the constitution—though we should have an election now to get a legitimate government—and then again an election in 1997 when the Canal is due to revert to Panama. But the United States will make sure there is still a docile government here. That government can abrogate the treaty, say it's too difficult for us little people to manage, please stay. The Canal isn't the important thing; it's the Canal Zone, the bases, the airfields. The United States dominates all Central America now and geographically Panama is the ideal control point.'

The Canal Zone is a strip of land north of Panama City ten miles wide by fifty miles long, between the Pacific and the Caribbean. It contains the Canal, the extensive civilian administration of the Canal, and a major US military installation, plus all their dependents and recreational facilities. By the terms of the 1977 Panama Canal treaty, this will be ceded back to Panama in 1999 and the treaty forbids the presence of foreign troops on Panamanian soil.

The Invasion was obviously long-planned, waiting for a 'Just Cause', and Noriega, crazy with hubris, obliged. President Carter had forced through the Panama Canal Treaty; it had never suited the military or the Republicans and no doubt they would like to cancel it if they can. Still, nothing explains the preposterous size of the Invasion, the most copious display of force since Vietnam. Unless Operation Just Cause was intended as a very special PR job: to remind every country from the Caribbean basin to the Strait of Magellan that the United States is the last superpower.

My Panamanian journalist colleagues also gave me a sheaf of documents, press releases from various unions and the American Independent Commission of Inquiry on the US Invasion of Panama. The unions accuse the Endara government of denying their rights, won during twenty-one years of dictatorship. The Independent Commission accuses the US government of 'police state tactics', citing cases. The arrest by American soldiers of Dr Romulo Escobar Betancourt, chief negotiator of the Panama Canal Treaty, formerly Chancellor of Panama University and delegate to the UN, who was held incommunicado for five days at Fort Clayton, then turned over to the Panamanian police. The ongoing searches, harassments and interrogation of Panamanian civilians by US military. The arrest order for seventy-four prominent Panamanians, known as lifelong supporters of Panamanian independence, to be charged with 'impeding the renewal of the Powers of the State.' The penalty is five to twenty years in prison and prohibition from holding public office. The Independent Commission concludes that there is 'a clear and continuing effort by the United States government to intimidate and crush any democratic opposition.'

The Spanish word for totally destitute is *damnificado*. The people who ran from their burning collapsing houses in Chorrillo, with the clothes on their backs, saving their lives and nothing else, were *los damnificados de Chorrillo*. I wanted to hear their stories, exactly what happened on the night of the Invasion and what was happening to them now. The Panamanian journalists said they were not allowed to see them; maybe I could get in.

Three thousand *damnificados* are housed at an unused US airfield. The US army built windowless plywood cubicles for most of them in an unused hangar. The cubicles are three metres by three metres. The high, shadowed building is at least cool; the overflow suffocates in army tents. Another 500 *damnificados* camp in two city schools.

I got to the hangar entrance and was stopped. As I had no press credentials of any kind, I made a bullying scene, saying that if I could not speak to these refugees the authorities must have something to hide. The camp director, from the Panamanian Red Cross, conceded that he would let me in if the '*Señora*' the government representative, gave me a letter. I returned to Panama. After infuriating telephone calls, trying to find this lady, she appeared at my hotel, a nice oligarchy aristocrat. She wrote a note and telephoned the Red Cross director to expect me.

I went back. This time I got no farther than the guard post. The camp director came to meet me, all welcoming smiles, and took the note. But the American lieutenant on duty, eight feet tall, white, swathed in bandoliers, hefting his M-16 (a seriously threatening weapon) said: No. I did not have a 'seal' (a press card from Southern Command?); my name was not on his roster.

I observed that the Panamanian authority and the camp director gave me permission to talk to Panamanian citizens and I did not see what the US army had to do with it.

'Anybody can write a letter,' said the lieutenant, holding the note. 'I have my orders.' The camp director, who of course knew the handwriting and knew his superior had agreed to my visit, stood beside the lieutenant, looking at the ground. It was a public humiliation, delivered with indifference. US Southern Command rules, OK.

I said to the camp director, in Spanish, 'You live under an army of occupation.'

He closed his eyes for a second and said softly, 'What can we do?'

I said, 'You have my full sympathy.'

He said, 'Thank you, *Señora*,' and we shook hands.

I walked back to the warehouses where traffic was stopped and found a taxi that had just deposited a passenger, which spared me the long, hot trudge to the main road and a bus. A very young woman, very pregnant, asked for a lift to town. We sat in the back with her five-year-old son between us. The boy was much too thin, pale, dressed in a clean, pressed white shirt and cotton trousers. By chance, I learned from this tired, helpless girl what I had wanted to know. Her story was brief.

'I grabbed the child and we ran through the bullets. We ran and ran until we came to the sea. Now something is bad with baby,' she touched her stomach. 'I must go to the hospital every day. My father gives me two dollars for the taxis. He is a taxi driver. I have no money or anything. Many people were burned up, many, many, old ones and children who could not get out. At the camp they give us coffee and dry bread for breakfast and at five in the afternoon one plate of food.' She sighed and looked at the boy. He sat on the edge of the seat, rigid and silent. 'He is very nervous. If there is the smallest noise, he trembles and cries.'

She had been there in one of those big wood boxes when suddenly her home, her neighbourhood, blazed with fire, and the people tried to escape 'through the bullets'. Her testimony was the reason why Southern Command prevented journalists from meeting the *damnificados*. She cannot have been a special case. All the uprooted survivors of Chorrillo lived through the same fearful night.

We dropped her at the hospital. I wished her luck, wondering what that might be. Not to die in childbirth? Not to produce a deformed or deranged baby?

I went to my room, showered, and drank duty-free whiskey, raging against the Divine Right of US Presidents to do anything they like to poor people in Central America. This arrogance derives from the Monroe Doctrine of 1823, which is no more than a Presidential fiat warning the European powers not to meddle in the

Americas. The United States would then refrain from meddling in Europe. Ever since, US Presidents have meddled ceaselessly in the affairs of sovereign states, south of the US border.

South American states, though tightly entangled in debt to North America, are by now very prickly. After the CIA orchestration of the demise of President Allende of Chile, US Presidents are not apt to interfere flagrantly in South America. But Central America could be described as a free fire zone. Anything goes.

Why have the leaders, the media, the citizens of the Great Western Democracies cared long and ardently for the people of Central Europe, but cared nothing for the people of Central America? Between twenty-seven and twenty-eight million people live in the seven states of Central America. Most of them are bone poor, and most of them do not have white skin. Their lives and their deaths have not touched the conscience of the world. I can testify that it was far better and safer to be a peasant in communist Poland than it is to be a peasant in capitalist El Salvador.

US Presidents, who formulate US foreign policy, never worried about social justice in Central America. The White House tolerates any Central American government if it is loyal to the ideology of capitalism and knows its place, subservience to the national interests of the United States as defined in Washington. Washington likes dictators because they are easier to deal with. US Presidents regularly clamp down on popular rebellions. The demand of cruelly deprived people for a decent life is seen as dangerous to US interests; quite simply, the poor are dangerous. They are capable of saying: Yank Go Home.

No US President ever deposed a dictatorship in Central America or South America either. On the contrary. Noriega is unique. Noriega would still be there if he had not fancied he could be an independent dictator; the fool got above himself. The drug business will continue; North Americans want drugs; drug money will be laundered discreetly. But everything is in order now; the US has taken over Panama in its usual style, with a friendly native government. 'Democracy', which has the sound of silver bells in Central Europe, is a mean joke in Central America.

On the western arm of the Bay of Panama, a forest of condominium skyscrapers rises from untended land. No trees, bushes, flowers, just these massive vulgar buildings. Nearby, luxurious houses are screened by large delightful gardens. This neighbourhood is the golden ghetto of Paitilla, the habitat of the class that the people call *la oligarquía*, the winners of the Invasion.

That night there was a lecture, with three speakers, at the Marriott Caesar Park Hotel, the biggest, gaudiest, most expensive hotel in Panama. It was an oligarchy event. The audience sat in a grandiose salon and listened with rapt attention to two lectures, read by important Panamanians. The subject was: 'Democracy, Sovereignty and Invasion.' The audience, perhaps a hundred people, was mostly men, mostly overweight, wearing good dark suits. Noriega, like Torrijos before him, never touched their money or their lifestyle. But for twenty-one years, they were shelved: they had no active role in government. And they were shamed; it was shaming to be citizens of a state ruled by a squalid crook from the gutter. Upper class Panamanians were the dissidents here. Overnight, literally, Operation Just Cause solved their problems.

The tone of the lectures was creamy satisfaction. To stay awake, I made notes among which I find the well-turned phrase 'pseudo-intellectual bullshit'. Neither speaker mentioned the dead, the homeless, the bankrupted small businesses. I wondered if any of them had looked at the wasteland of Chorrillo. The general sense was clear enough: the Endara government was just fine; the United States was just fine; all was again right with their world.

After two long lectures, the audience needed a rest. They moved to the hall and the meeting became a cocktail party, with drinks from a bar set up for the occasion. The women, now on view, were very chic, in traditional smart little black dresses and appropriate jewellery. Everyone knew everyone else and everyone was white, the flower of Panamanian society.

After the intermission the last speaker was introduced, to applause, as 'the next President of Cuba'. He told his reverent audience that democracy was fragile; Noriegismo was not dead; they must be vigilant to protect their regained freedom. Then he said that Latin America would not have objected to the Invasion if it hadn't been done by the United States. Very odd. Who else would have done it? He ended with an impassioned plea for the liberty of Cuba. Was he urging a US Invasion there? A bloodbath for his countrymen? They gave the next President of Cuba a standing ovation. Some of those here tonight had been in exile in the United States for eight months, from last May—when Noriega violently broke up the election that was going against him—until the December Invasion. But this Cuban had lived in exile in Spain for thirty years; he was their hero.

The University of Panama made a pleasing contrast to the Marriott Park Caesar. It is a sprawl of grimily white cement buildings, inside and out a basic factory for learning. But the buildings, planted in a lovely jungle of trees and flowering shrubs, are linked by colonnaded shady walkways and the kids look bright and shabby and it is a good place. Ten thousand young men and women study here in three daily shifts which start at seven a.m. and end at midnight. Tuition ranges from thirty to forty-five dollars a semester; law and medicine cost the most.

Each faculty has a students' association, with elected officers. I was looking for Literature and found Psychology. The three officers of their students' association sat with me in an enlarged cubby-hole off the small study room; they closed the door. They took turns talking, in low voices as if we were conspirators.

The tall, pale blond said, 'We can say things here we would not say in public. People are afraid to talk. Some professors are in favour of this government. It is bourgeois; all of them born rich; there is no new young blood. When the United States hit us with the embargo we managed anyway; it didn't crush us. The idea of needing identity papers signed by a *norteamericano* general is repugnant.'

The small plump dark one said, 'We are all anti-Noriega but Noriega brought up working class men and gave them positions of power. That was good. This government will keep its own class in the top jobs. We don't think this is democracy. We are nationalists, we want to govern our country in our own way.'

The other dark boy said, 'In this university it doesn't matter if you are the son of a taxi driver or a cabinet minister's son. I think the Invasion was wrong and we ought to have a free election, not this government. The curfew is spoiling our lives. We always went to each other's houses and listened to music and talked or we went to cafés or danced. Now we can't be out after nine o'clock for fear of running into anti-socials or gringo military patrols.'

I asked about drugs; after all, the Invasion was supposed to be about drugs. According to President Bush, drugs are America's number one enemy, threatening its youth, its future, and drugs are not unknown in American universities. They agreed that there were no drugs on the campus and never had been. 'People are motivated to study, the blond said, 'or they wouldn't be here.'

I went to the Law faculty next day, thinking that these future lawyers were most apt to be future politicians. A small, thin young man, elected representative of the law students' association, spoke in a guarded voice. Strangely cautious, like the psychology students: 'All of us here are against the Invasion. The vote last May was against Noriega but not for Endara. We should have had an election now; this is not a legal government. We are not hopeful of the future. We do not think the law will be independent and honest with this government. Already they are appointing judges, magistrates, in the same manner as Noriega, their friends, their relatives. Not on merit. I doubt if there will be an honourable system of justice in Panama for a long time.'

Pedro was the most interesting of the many interesting taxi drivers. I always sat in front, for leg room and conversation. On my last day in Panama, Pedro agreed to drive me around Chorrillo for an hour; many would not, due to the robbery syndrome. Pedro was a little, under-nourished, monkeyish mulatto aged twenty-five or thirty-five. He wore a fixed dazzling smile, as if his face had frozen into this hilarity. Driving down Via España, he said, 'At ten-thirty that night I was stopped by soldiers back there.'

'What soldiers?' The Invasion started after midnight.

'Panamanians. They were stopping cars to carry munitions from their Cuartel to the Cuartel in Chorrillo. but my taxi was too small. One of them fired a shot in the air and said, "Get out!" I tell you the truth, my heart was in my hands! I drove home as fast as possible. I was so full of fear that I stayed there for three days.'

'They knew about the Invasion then?'

'Clearly. But the people did not believe it until they heard the bombs.' We were now in the area of devastation. 'That was the

Photo: James Nachtwey (Magnum)

gymnasium for Noriega's officers.' A big building, parts of the walls still standing; inside you could see what had been a basketball court. An old woman sat in the doorway. We drove slowly through the grey wasteland. It had been possible to raze only the stumps of the wood tenements. They must have dynamited the remains of Noriega's Cuartel headquarters.

Pedro stopped before another large building. 'It was three storeys high.'

From what I have seen in war, this building took a direct heavy bomb hit. Nothing else would scoop it out, leaving only jagged sections of wall. *Army*, which gives the most detailed record of Operation Just Cause, states that Stealth fighter planes, used here for the first time, dropped 'concussion bombs'. So we know that planes were in action, and 'concussion bombs' sounds like a cover-up.

'It was a reform school,' Pedro said. 'Boys and girls from five to seventeen. The Cuartel was over there, behind it.'

'They were sleeping here?'

'They were sleeping here.'

I do not see how any of the children could have survived.

'Sad,' Pedro said, his smile brilliant, his voice grieving.

'Let's go,' I said. 'It makes me sick.'

We passed empty yellow tower-blocks, like Juan's, and studied a huge hole near ground-level in a blank side of one building. The burn marks on upper floors were understandable: rockets. I could not guess the purpose of the hole, about five feet in diameter, nor what made it; perhaps some new super-bazooka. 'This is the Model Prison,' Pedro said. 'Look at the wall.' A high solid steel wall surrounds the prison; it too was pierced by a huge hole. 'All the prisoners escaped,' Pedro said, 'now there are other prisoners.'

On a street below the prison, Pedro said, 'This is the School of the Saviour. More than 300 people who lost their homes in Chorrillo live here.' The school had been painted dark red with yellow trim long ago. On the cement front yard, half-naked unwashed kids played and shrieked. Women leaned from the windows shouting at their children and each other. It was very hot. Pedro wiped his face again with a wet grey rag. You could imagine the smell of the place. Being an old slum school, it would have a few old toilets and wash-basins. Across the street the little looted shops were boarded up, except for a re-opened corner grocery store.

'Sad, sad,' Pedro said.

'Yes, but at least they aren't guarded by American soldiers. They can make all the noise they want,' for suddenly I remembered the unnatural stillness in the hangar. 'They can walk to the centre of town; they're in their own neighbourhood.'

'It takes much time for poor people to gain possessions. Then everything they possessed is gone, like that, in a minute. And, who knows, relatives too. Where their houses were they see there is nothing.' He turned his frantic smile and his sorrowful eyes to me, making sure I understood. 'Nothing like this ever happened in Panama. Never.'

JONATHAN RABAN
NEW WORLD

Seattle, circa 1900.

It's dark and deathly quiet in here. The sheets of the bed are cool and laundry-smelling, but there's a niff in the air, sweet and sickly, like dead chrysanthemums. Sleep has disassembled the self: it will take patience to rebuild a person out of the heap of components in the bed. The dial of a wrist-watch looms in front of a single open eye; its luminous green hands say that it is either twenty-five after midnight or five in the morning. The spare human hand goes out on a cautious reconnaissance patrol through the darkness. It snags on a sharp corner, knocks over a bottle of pills, finds a solid, cold ceramic bulge. Fingers close on the knurled screw of the switch, and the room balloons with light.

It's a conventioneers' hotel room. The waking eye takes in the clubland furniture in padded leatherette, the Audubon prints, the thirty-six inch TV mounted over the mini-bar, the heavy cream drapes across the window. The room is painlessly impersonal, artfully designed to tell the self nothing about where it is or who it is supposed to be. It looks like its price. It is just a seventy-five dollar room.

The nose sources the bad smell to a tooth-glass of scotch and tap-water on the bedside table. The time is five o'clock but feels later.

Does seventy-five dollars buy twenty-four-hour room service? The shallow drawer below the telephone ought to yield a hotel directory, but doesn't. It contains two books of the same size and in the same binding: a Gideon Bible and *The Teaching of Buddha*, in English and Japanese, donated (it says) by the Buddhist Promoting Foundation, Japan. This is the room's first and only giveaway. The hotel where Jesus and Buddha live side by side in the drawer is on the Pacific Rim. The text is printed on thin crinkly paper.

> A true homeless brother determines to reach his goal of Enlightenment even though he loses his last drop of blood and his bones crumble into powder. Such a man, trying his best, will finally attain the goal and give evidence of it by his ability to do the meritorious deeds of a homeless brother.

There's no reply from room service on 107, so, sitting up in bed, long before dawn and *Good Morning America*, I read Gautama for the first time and find his teaching interestingly apposite to the situation and the hour.

Unenlightened man, said the Buddha, was trapped in an endless cycle of becoming—always trying to be something else or somebody else. His unhappy fate was to spend eternity passing from one incarnation to the next, each one a measure of his ignorant restlessness and discontent. In the search for Nirvana, man must stop being a becomer and learn how to be a be–er.

It is a profoundly un-American philosophy. Here in this travellers' room, in this nation of chronic travellers and becomers, *The Teaching of Buddha* strikes the same note of disregarded truth as the health warning on an emptied pack of cigarettes. The idea that the whole of the external world is a treacherous fiction, that the self has no real existence, goes right against the Protestant, materialist American grain.

No wonder that so many Americans have looked across the Pacific to Buddhism to provide an antidote to the American condition. Emerson and the New England Transcendentalists—Whitman—T. S. Eliot—the Dharma Bums—J. D. Salinger—Robert M. Pirsig's *Zen and the Art of Motorcycle Maintenance*: in every phase of post-colonial American history, Buddhism has offered a rhetoric of dissent; and on the Pacific coast it has coloured the fabric of the culture.

I look at the advice I've failed to follow—

> In the evening he should have a time for quiet sitting and meditation and a short walk before retiring. For peaceful sleep he should rest on the right side with his feet together and his last thought should be of the time when he wishes to rise in the early morning.

—and copy it into my notebook. It sounds like a good tip; far better than pills and whisky.

Fiction or not, the external world is beginning to make its presence felt now. The drapes open on a city still blue in the half-light. Lines of cars on the wet streets a few floors below the window are making a muffled drumming sound; the morning commute from the suburbs is already under way. Seven o'clock. It's time to shave and shower; time to put Buddha back in the drawer and become someone else.

On that particular morning, in hotels and motels, in furnished rooms and cousins' houses, 106 other people were waking to their first day as immigrants to Seattle. These were flush times, with jobs to be had for the asking, and the city was growing at the rate of nearly 40,000 new residents a year. The immigrants were piling in from every quarter. Many were out-of-state Americans: New Yorkers on the run from the furies of Manhattan; refugees from the Restbelt; Los Angelenos escaping their infamous crime statistics, huge house-prices and jammed and smoggy freeways; redundant farm workers from Kansas and Iowa. Then there were the Asians—Samoans, Laotians, Cambodians, Thais, Vietnamese, Chinese and Koreans, for whom Seattle was the nearest city in the continental United States. A local artist had proposed a monumental sculpture, to be put up at the entrance to Elliott Bay, representing Liberty holding aloft a bowl of rice.

The falling dollar, which had so badly hurt the farming towns of the Midwest, had come as a blessing to Seattle. It lowered the price abroad of the Boeing airplanes, wood pulp, paper, computer software and all the other things that Seattle manufactured. The port of Seattle was a day closer by sea to Tokyo and Hong Kong than was Los Angeles, its main rival for the shipping trade with Asia.

By the end of the 1980s, Seattle had taken on the dangerous lustre of a promised city. The rumour had gone out that if you had failed in Detroit you might yet succeed in Seattle—and that if you'd succeeded in Seoul, you could succeed even better in Seattle. In New York and in Guntersville I'd heard the rumour. Seattle was the coming place.

So I joined the line of hopefuls.

Of all the new arrivals, it was the Koreans who had made the biggest, boldest splash. Wherever I went, I saw their patronyms on storefronts, and it seemed that half the small family businesses in Seattle were owned by Parks or Kims. I picked up my trousers from the dry cleaner's at the back of the Josephinum, stopped for milk and eggs at a Korean corner grocery, looked through the steamy window of a Korean tailor's, passed the Korean wig shop on Pike Street, bought oranges, bananas and grapes from a Korean fruit stall in the market, and walked the hundred yards home via a Korean laundromat and a Korean news and candy kiosk.

For lunch I went to Shilla, where I sat up at the bar, ordered a beer, and tried to make sense of the newspaper which had been left on the counter—the *Korea Times*, published daily in Seattle. The text was in Korean characters, but the pictures told one something. There were portrait photographs of beaming Korean–American businessmen dressed, like many of the restaurant's customers, in blazers, button-down shirts and striped club ties. Several columns were devoted to prize students, shown in their mortar boards and academic gowns. On page three there was a church choir. There was a surprising number of advertisements for pianos. I guessed that the tone of the text would be inspirational and uplifting: the *Korea Times* seemed to be exclusively devoted to the cult of business, social and academic success.

'You are reading our paper!' It was the proprietor of the restaurant, a wiry man with a tight rosebud smile.

'No—just looking at the pictures.'

He shook my hand, sat on the stool beside me and showed me the paper page by page. Here was the news from Korea; this was local news from Seattle and Tacoma; that was Pastor Kim's family advice column; these were the advertisements for jobs . . .

'It is very important to us. Big circulation! Everybody read it!'

So, nearly a hundred years ago, immigrant Jews in New York had pored over the *Jewish Daily Forward*, the *Yidishe Gazetn* and the *Arbeite Tseitung*. They had kept their readers in touch with the news and culture of the old world at the same time as they had taught the immigrants how to make good in the new. To the greenhorn American, the newspaper came as a daily reassurance that he was not alone.

'You are interested?' the restaurateur said. 'You must talk to Mr Han. He is the president of our association. He is here—'

Mr Han was eating by himself, hunched over a plate of seafood. In sweatshirt and windbreaker, he had the build of a bantamweight boxer. The proprietor introduced us. Mr Han bowed from his seat, waved his chopsticks. Sure! No problem! Siddown!

His face looked bloated with fatigue. His eyes were almost completely hidden behind pouches of flesh, giving him the shuttered-in appearance of a sleep-walker. But his mouth was wide awake, and there was a surviving ebullience in his grin, which was unselfconsciously broad and toothy.

He gave me his card. Mr Han was President of the Korean Association of Seattle, also owner of Japanese Auto Repair ('is *big* business!'). He had been in America, he said, for sixteen years. He'd made it. But his college-student clothes, his twitchy hands and the knotted muscles in his face told another story. If you passed Mr Han on the street, you'd mistake him for a still shell-shocked newcomer; an F.O.B., as people said even now, long after the Boeing had displaced the immigrant ship. He looked fresh-off-the-boat.

It had been the summer of 1973 when Won S. Han had flown from Seoul to Washington D.C. with 400 dollars in his billfold and a student visa in his passport. He had come to study Psychology—that was what his papers said, at least—but what he really wanted to major in was the applied science of becoming an American.

In Korea, he had been brought up as a Buddhist. Within two weeks of his arrival in Washington, he was a Baptist.

'Yah! I become Christian! I didn't go to church to believe in God, not then, no. I go to church for meeting people. Yah. Baptist church was where to find job, where to find place to live, where to find wife, husband, right? In America, you gotta be Christian!' His voice was lippy, whispery, front-of-the-mouth.

He'd soon fallen behind in his Psychology classes. He couldn't follow the strange language. Through the church, he found a part-time job in a gas- and service-station. He learned the work easily. While the American workers were content to lounge and smoke and tinker, this university-educated Korean gutted the car manuals and took only a few weeks to qualify as a full-fledged auto mechanic.

'We are hot-temper people! Want to do things quick-quick-quick! Not slow-slow like in America. Want everything all-at-once, but in America you must learn to wait long-time. Quick-quick is the Korean way, but that's not work here. America teaches patience, teaches wait-till-next-week.'

This must have been a hard lesson for Mr Han to take to heart. He'd done a major reconstruction job on the American language to give it a greater turn of speed, lopping off articles, prepositions, all the fancy chromework of traditional syntax. His stripped-down English was now wonderfully fast and fluent. With its rat-a-tat-tat hyphenations and bang! bang! repetitions, it was a vehicle custom-built for its owner—a Korean racing machine in which Mr Han drove with his foot on the floor, without regard for petty American traffic restrictions.

Working as a mechanic by day, he'd gone to school at night. This time his subject was real-estate, and it took him six months to qualify for a Maryland realtor's licence. He gave up the car business and sold suburban houses, mostly to Korean customers.

'You know, when Korean guy come to this country, he has *plan*! In two year, must have own business. In three year, must have own house. Three year! Four at *maximum*. So must work-work-work. Sixteen-hour-day, eighteen-hour-day . . . OK, he can do. But *must* have business, *must* have house.'

Mr Han himself had run ahead of schedule. By 1982, when he left Washington and headed for Seattle, he was a man of capital with a wife and two young daughters. To begin with, he patrolled the city from end to end by car, casing the joint for opportunities.

'And you liked what you saw?'

'Yah! I like the mountains! Like the water! Like the trees! Is like in Korea, but not too hot, not too cold. *Nice*! No people! Green!'

Everywhere he'd gone, he'd checked in with the local Parks and Kims and got the low-down on Seattle's social structure. Beacon Hill, just south of downtown, was where Korean beginners started their American lives; as they succeeded, so they moved further north, to Queen Anne and Capitol Hill, across Lake Washington to Bellevue, across Lake Union to Wallingford, Morningside, Greenwood, North Beach. They measured the tone of a neighbourhood by the reputation of its schools. The top suburb was the one with the best record of posting students to famous American colleges like Columbia, Yale and M.I.T.

On his first day in Seattle, Mr Han had learned that the Shoreline School District was 'much better, no comparison!' than the Seattle School District, and that the Syre Elementary School was just the place for his daughters to set foot on the ladder to academic stardom. So he bought a house in Richmond Beach. He had no Korean neighbours. The closeness of the house to the school was all that mattered.

Then he set up his business.

'Must be *specialist!*' Mr Han said. Detroit was sick, and more and more Americans were buying Japanese cars, so Mr Han established his hospital for Japanese cars only. 'No American cars! No German! No English!—sorry! Must be Japanese. Toyota, Nissan, Mitsubishi, whatever. So long as it made in Japan—bring it in! That is my speciality.'

The climax of this success story had happened two years ago. Mr Han had always dreamed of having a son to carry on the Han dynastic name. In Korea, it was a woman's highest duty to give birth to a son. Mr Han himself was the only son of an only son—a man genetically programmed to produce a male heir. But it seemed that he could only father daughters. This was, he said, a heavy fate for a Korean man to shoulder.

'So, in 1986, I go to my wife. I say to her, 'One last try!' And we try. And—*Home Run!*' For the first time, Mr Han's eyes were wide open, his pride in this feat of paternity matched by this rich nugget of all-American slang.

'Home run!' He smacked his lips around the phrase and laughed, a joyful *hoo! hoo!* that made neighbouring diners look up from their tables.

'Now the name of Han goes on!'

With his business in the city, his civic honours in the Korean community, his big house in a wooded, crimeless suburb a spit away from the sea, his straight-A daughters and his precious son, one might have expected Mr Han to have grown expansive and complacent in his New World estate. Yet his eyes closed as quickly as they had opened; he fell back into hunched vigilance; he looked, as I had first seen him, like an anxious greener who fears that someone, somewhere, is hard on his heels.

He was frightened for his children.

'They see the American TV . . . of this I am scared. I turn off the news. There is too much immorality! violence! drugs! sex! When the news comes up—"Turn that TV off!"'

He had tried to turn his home into a Korean bubble, sealed off from the dangerous American world outside. In the house, the

239

family talked in Korean. Twice a week, the girls went to a Korean church school to take classes in Korean grammar and composition.

He dreaded the day when one of his daughters would bring home a white American boy-friend.

'What would you do?'

'Any kid of mine, I'd stop her marrying another race.'

'*Stop!*'

'Maybe could not *stop*. Maybe. But not *like*. You heard of "G.I. Brides" . . . They were not normal average Korean woman. They were—I not say exactly what they were, but you know what I mean.' Mr Han watched me across the table through his nearly closed eyes. 'Whores,' he said, making the word sound biblical.

I said that the Jews in New York at the beginning of the century had felt much as he did. But they had had the protection of the ghetto. In the Yiddish-speaking world of the Lower East Side, with its all-Jewish streets and all-Jewish schools, it was possible to regard the *goyim* as unmarriageable aliens. In Richmond Beach, a Korean girl would be a Christian, like most of her classmates, and her skin-colour would be hardly less pale than theirs. How, growing up in English, could she hug 'Koreanness' to herself as the essence of her identity, while all the time her parents talked Columbia, talked medical school, talked her up the path that led to membership of the white, professional, American middle class?

'Ah,' said Mr Han. 'This is what we are wondering. Wondering-wondering all the time. *How long*? is the question. In near future, next generation, we got to be serviced by English. We have example of Chinese. Look at Chinese!—in two-three generations, the Chinese people here, they cannot even read the characters! Chinese is only *name*. Is nothing. Now, Chinese . . . all in the melting pot!' He drew out this last phrase with solemn relish. The way he said it, it was a *mel Ting pot*, and I saw it as some famous cast-iron oriental cooking utensil, in which human beings were boiled over a slow fire until they broke down into a muddy fibrous stew.

'But my kids grow like Koreans,' Mr Han said.

'With American voices, American clothes, American college degrees . . .'

'Like Koreans.'

On the street across from the restaurant I could see a rambling black-painted chalet surmounted by a flying hoarding which said LOOK WHAT WE GOT! 30 NUDE SHOWGIRLS! TABLE DANCING! It was a sign to chill the heart of a Korean father of young daughters.

Since so much of American culture was clearly a Caucasian affront to Korean ideas of modesty, industry, piety and racial purity, I wondered why they kept on coming—from a country that was being touted as the economic miracle of the decade.

Mr Han guffawed when I said 'economic miracle'.

'Guy in Korea make three-four-hundred dollar a month. No house his own, no business his own. *This* is country of opportunity. No comparison. Chance of self-employment: maybe one thousand per cent better! Look. Seventy-three. I am in Washington, D.C. with four hundred dollars. Now? My business is worth one million dollars—more than one million. Heh? Isn't that the American Dream? And I am only a small! Yes, I am a *small*.'

Minutes later, I watched him as he crossed to his car. The millionaire was walking quick-quick-quick, shoulders hunched, head down, his skinny hands rammed deep into the pockets of his workpants. He looked like a man who had taken on America single-handed and, in the ninth round, was just winning, by a one- or two-point margin.

The Chinese had been the first Asians to make a new life in Seattle. They called America 'The Gold Mountain' and were eager to take on the hard, poorly paid jobs that were offered to them in the railroad construction gangs. For as long as it took to build the railroads, they were made welcome, in a mildly derisive way. Their entire race was renamed 'John', and every John was credited with an extraordinary capacity to do the maximum amount of work on the minimum amount of rice. As soon as the railroads began to lay off workers, the amiable John was reconceived as 'a yellow rascal' and 'the rat-eating Chinaman'. During the 1870s, the federal legislature began to behave towards the Chinese much as the Tsars Alexander II and Nicholas II behaved towards the Jews in Russia. At the very moment when the United States was receiving the European huddled masses on its eastern seaboard, it was establishing something cruelly like its own Pale, designed to exclude the Chinese from white American rights and occupations. The Geary Act prohibited the Chinese from the right to bail and habeas corpus. In Seattle in 1886, gangs of vigilantes succeeded in forcibly deporting most of the city's Chinese population of 350 people; persuading them, with knives, clubs and guns, to board a ship bound for San Francisco.

For the immigrant from Asia, the Gold Mountain was a treacherous rock-face. No sooner had you established what seemed to be a secure foothold than it gave way under you. The treatment of the Seattle Chinese in 1886 was matched, almost exactly, by the treatment of the Seattle Japanese in 1942, when hundreds of families were arrested, loaded on trains and despatched to remote internment camps.

Now, if you came from Asia, you could not trust America to be kind or fair. This particular week, if you went to an English class at the Central Community College, you would see spray-gunned on the south wall of the building SPEAK ENGLISH OR DIE, SQUINTY EYE! Peeing in a public toilet, you'd find yourself stuck, for the duration with a legend written just for you: KILL THE GOOKS

In the ghetto of Seattle's International District, a four-by-four block grid of morose, rust-coloured tenements, there was at least safety in numbers. There was less pressure on the immigrant to get his tongue round the alien syllables of English. Even a professional man, like the dentist or optometrist, could conduct his business entirely in his original language. In the bar of the China Gate restaurant, I sat next to a man in his early seventies, born on Jackson Street, who had served with the United States Air Force in World War Two. He was affable, keen to tell me about his travels and almost completely incomprehensible, *Yi wong ding ying milding hyall!*

'You were in Mildenhall? In Suffolk?'

'Yea! Milding Hall!'

So, painfully, we swapped memories of the air base there. He didn't understand much of what I said, and I didn't understand much of what he said; yet his entire life, bar this spell in wartime England, had been passed in Seattle—or, rather, within the Chinese-speaking fifty-acre grid.

The Chinese, the Japanese, the Vietnamese, Laotians and Cambodians had all established solid fortresses in, or on the edge of, the International District. There were few Koreans here. There was the Korean Ginseng Center on King Street; there was a Korean restaurant at the back of the Bush Hotel on Jackson; some Koreans worked as bartenders in the Chinese restaurants.

In Los Angeles, there was a 'Little Korea'; a defined area of the city where the immigrant could work for, and live with, his co-linguists, much as the Chinese did here in the International District. For Koreans in Seattle, though, immigration was, for nearly everyone, a solitary process. The drive to own their own businesses, to send their children to good schools, to have space, privacy, self-sufficiency, had scattered them, in small family groups of twos and threes, through the white suburbs. They didn't have the daily solace of the sociable rooming house, the street and the café. For many, there was the once-a-week visit to church; for others, there was no Korean community life at all.

It was this solitude that drew me to them. The Seattle Koreans knew, better than anyone else, what it was like to go it alone in America; and although I came from the wrong side of the world I could feel a pang of kinship for these people who had chosen to travel by themselves.

Everyone could name the date on which they'd taken the flight out from Seoul. The beginning of their American life was at least as important to them as their birthday.

'August twenty-ninth, 1965,' Jay Park said. He owned a plumbing business up on Beacon Hill and drove a pearl-grey '88 Mercedes. In 1965, he'd been twenty; and on that August afternoon he'd stood in Seoul airport being hugged by every aunt, cousin, uncle, friend.

'Everyone envy me. It was like I'd won the big lottery, you know? I'd got the visa! Wah! They was seeing me off like I was some general . . . like I was going into Paradise!'

Park knew America. He'd 'watched it through the movies'. On the streets of Seoul, he'd seen 'US soldiers spending money like it was going out of style. Wah! I tell you, the US was like a paradise. You feel like you're going to dreamland. Everything's going to work out OK!'

It was a Northwest Airlines flight; Jay Park had never been on an airplane before and he had 'not one word' of English. The stewardess showed him to an aisle seat, next to an American who was reading a book.

'He don't look at me. I felt shy. Suddenly I was kind of scared, the excitement was overwhelming. This guy was reading his book, so I read the in-flight magazine. I mean, not *read*, but made out like I was reading. I was just looking at the pictures of the US, but I was taking a long time over every one, so this guy would think I could read the English.'

The plane took off. 'No problem,' but Jay Park wished he could see out the window. He didn't dare to lean across the body of his American neighbour; so, holding the magazine close to his face, he'd sneaked glances—seen jigsaw puzzle bits of city and mountain slide past the lozenge of perspex as the plane banked.

A meal was served. 'That was real great! American food! I was in the US already!'

At Tokyo they had stopped to refuel. Jay Park was in an agony of impatience. Other Koreans on the flight were buying watches and radios at the Tokyo duty-free shop, but Jay Park sat fretting on a bench during the stopover, his mind full of America.

Then came the long haul across the Pacific. They left the sunset behind—Park could see it gleaming gold on the trailing edge of the plane's starboard wing—and flew into the night. He remembered the blinds being pulled down for the projection of the movie. With no headset, he could only watch the pictures—more postcards of America. 'Oh boy! *Dis* is where I'm goin'! I'm in the movie!'

Exhausted by his excitement, he fell asleep. When he woke up, the quick night was already over. Time itself was whizzing by faster than the clouds below, but the plane was still a long way from America. The morning lasted forever. 'Then—they were saying something through the speaker, but my ears were blocking up. *Seattle!* That's all I hear. *Seattle!*'

There was nothing to see. America was a huge grey cloud, through which the plane was making its unbearably slow descent. When it touched down, Jay Park was high, in a toxic trance.

'Wah! Man! The airport! When you're walking through, your mind is set, "*This is America!*" Everything is *nice! great! fantasy!*'

The air inside the terminal was magic air. It smelled of cologne and money. There were advertising posters for things—'I don't know what they are, but, boy, they look good to me!'

The two hours he spent standing in line, waiting to be processed by the immigration officials, were precious, American hours. 'No, I don't care! I just think, Wah! I'm in the US!'

His sponsors were waiting for him in the arrivals lobby, a Korean-American couple in their forties who had been friends of his parents back in Seoul. Jay Park had never met them before, but they were holding up a sheet of cardboard with his name on it.

'Oh, but they'd done *great!* I was expecting them to take me in a bus, but they got their own car! A Chevy. Blue. Musta been a '63, '64 model. Yeah. Nice long sheer, box type, really fancy! You sitting in the back seat, looking out, it *astounds*. Wow! All the freeways, all the cars!'

The blue Chevy drove north, up the I-5 towards Seattle.

'*Whassat?* Hey, goddam, *whassat?*'

Jay Park saw a great factory—but it wasn't a factory; it was a supermarket. He loved the huge pictures raised over the six-lane highway, the smoking cowboys, the girls in swimsuits. *Wah! America!*

'Then, passing the downtown, *goddam!* The Smith Tower! The Space Needle! Godawmighty! You gotta *look* at that! But so few people! There was hardly any peoples was there! *No people, hardly.* You feel uneasy. *What's going on? Is the people all gone home?* This is real strange, not having people around. In Korea, people everywhere; in America—no people!'

The Chevy left the I-5 and headed up Aurora Avenue, along the wooded edge of Lake Union. It crossed the George Washington Bridge and entered the northern suburbs.

'It was the cleanness! The cars parked neatly! Just like the movies! And the lawns . . . No fences, no walls. In Korea, it was all high stone walls round every house. Here, is all open, all lawns, lawns, lawns. Looking out the car window, I see people's bikes left out front, just like that . . . like, here you can just leave things out overnight. No thieves! I think, *everything is coming true! What the movies say is true! This is like paradise is supposed to be!*'

His sponsors lived in a neat frame house in Greenwood.

'They had tables and chairs, the American way, not all on the floor like in Korea. Wah, man! I was cautious, then. Like, first thing, I want to use the toilet, you know? They show me where it is, and I spend a long, long time just looking around in there, Like, *If I use it, where's the smell going to go? Oh! I get it! There's the fan!* Stuff like that. Little things. Then they show me the bed where I'm to sleep? I never slept on a bed before. I think, *how you sleep on a bed without falling off?* I fell out of that bed a few times, too.'

That evening, his sponsors took Jay Park to the local supermarket.

'Wah! The steaks! The hamburgers! To eat a *whole* piece of meat! Even chickens! And they're so *cheap* too!'

He slept on the strange bed in a state of delirious wonder, his dreams far outclassed by America's incredible reality. In the morning, he ventured out into the backyard. A man—a white American—was pottering in the garden next door.

'He said to me, "Hi!" and then he said *something*. I didn't say anything. I think I give him a smile . . . I *hope* I give him a smile . . . then I go back into the house. *They speak English out there!*'

But: 'I was ready to tackle anything, anyhow.' With his sponsors' help, he enrolled for classes twice a week at the Central Community College. He got a job as a porter at a dry-ice factory. It paid $1.25 an hour—'great money!'. He found lodgings, with an Italian woman who worked at a downtown grocery and mothered him. Bed and board cost him thirty-five dollars a week; but as soon as work was over at the factory, Jay Park was out mowing people's lawns. If he put in a sixteen hour day, he could make 120 dollars in a week—a fortune. In his new Levis and his long-brimmed baseball cap, Jay Park was living the movie as he toted ice and mowed grass.

'Downtown, though, that was a big shock for me. You look—wah, godawmighty!—really strange people! Those poor whites, down in skid row? You never expecting skid row to exist in a country like this! I never seen *that* in the movies.'

He was having a hard time with the language. He went to his classes. He sat up late every night, slogging over his homework. He studied the programmes he saw on television, treating *Hogan's*

Heroes as a set text. 'I want something, I get it,' Jay Park said, but he couldn't get English.

'There was such pain building up inside me . . . People say things at work, I can't answer back! There's no *language* there! Nothing in the mouth! So you must make physical movement, you know? You get *violent!*'

So he punched and jabbed to make himself understood. Lost for a word, he socked the American air and laid it flat.

He was *making out.* He was saving. After a year of lawn-mowing and digging out borders, he was able to bill himself as 'Jay Park—Contractor and Landscape Gardener', but he was still travelling across Seattle by bus. It took him until 1967 before he'd put away enough to buy his first car.

'It was a 1960 T-Bird. Light blue. Electric windows and everything else. *You* owning own car, wah! that was a thrill, man.'

Now he drove his Italian landlady everywhere. She was chauffeured to work, chauffeured around the stores. Waiting for her, parked on the street, Jay Park, Contractor, Landscape Gardener, Ice Merchant, American, sat behind the wheel listening to the music of his electric windows buzzing up and down. 'Boy, I loved that car!'

Their experience had turned the immigrants into compulsive story-tellers. Much more than most people, they saw their own lives as having a narrative shape, a plot with a climactic dénouement. Each story was moulded by conventional rules. Korean men liked to see themselves as Horatio Alger heroes. Once upon a time there had been poverty, adversity, struggle. But character had triumphed over circumstance. The punchline of the story was 'Look at me now!', and the listener was meant to shake his head in admiration at the size of the business, the car, the house, at the school and college grades of the narrator's children, and at the amazing fortitude and pluck of the narrator, for having won so much in this country of opportunity. The story, in its simplest form, was a guileless tribute both to the virtues of the Korean male and to the bounty of America.

I preferred to listen to the stories of the women. They were closer to Flaubert than to Alger; their style was more realistic; they were more complicated in structure; they had more regard for pain and for failure.

Insook Webber took the flight for Seattle on 23 April 1977.

'I'd never been in an airplane before, but I loved—I absolutely adored—the idea of flying. I loved to see the planes in the sky. For me, they were flying into—like a fantasy world? A world of possibilities. And I had this premonition. It was always inside me, that somehow, someday, I'd leave Korea.'

She was in her thirties now, fine boned, fine skinned, her hair grown down to her shoulders in the American way. Her English was lightly, ambiguously, accented. In silk scarf and chunky cardigan, she looked dressed for a weekend in the Hamptons. She was married to an American; a Yale philosophy graduate who chose to work, unambitiously, in an accountants' office. She herself was a hospital nurse.

In 1977, Insook's elder sister had already been in America for five years, and Insook was going out to help look after her sister's children.

'I didn't know what to expect. I was totally open, totally vulnerable.'

'What did "America" mean?'

'America? It was a place in novels I'd read, and films I'd seen . . It was Scarlett O'Hara and *Gone With The Wind*. I was going to live at Tara and meet Rhett Butler, I guess . . . '

The flight itself was thrilling. Insook had a window seat; looking down on the clouds was how life was meant to be.

'I was breaking out all over with excitement. I was totally tired, but I couldn't sleep for a moment in case I missed something.'

It was after dark when the plane approached the coast. The sky was clear, and Insook's first glimpse of America was a lighted city.

'Like diamonds. Miles and miles of diamonds. I couldn't believe it—that people could afford so much *electricity*! We were having to save electricity in Korea then. I knew America was a rich country, but not *this* rich, to squander such a precious thing as electricity . . . I'd never dreamed of so many lights being switched on all at once.'

The plane landed at Sea-Tac, and it wasn't until past two a.m. that Insook was in possession of her green card, her ticket to becoming an American. Out in the concourse, she spotted her sister waiting for her, but her sister didn't recognize her.

'I was only fifteen when she left—still a kid. I was twenty now, and I'd grown. I had to *persuade* her I was me . . .'

Insook's scanty luggage was put aboard the family car, and they headed for the suburbs.

'Those huge wide roads, and huge lit-up signs . . . It made me feel very small . . . It was like being a little child again . . . Everything so big, so bright.'

She was describing the shock of being born.

Her sister's house was quiet. 'Too quiet. It was like the inside of a coffin. It wasn't like the real world . . .'

Nor was America. Insook was astounded and frightened by the extravagance of the country in which she found herself. When she went to a McDonalds, she wanted to take home the packaging of her hamburger and save it—it seemed criminal to simply throw it away in a litter-bin. A short walk on her first day took her from a rich neighbourhood into a poor one. 'On this street, these Americans live like kings—and on that, they are beggars! I thought, *My God, how can people* live *like this*? *How can they live* with *this*?'

Most immigrants were able to enjoy a few weeks, or days at least, of manic elation in the new country before depression hit them, as they woke up to the enormity of what they'd done. For Insook, the depression came at almost the same moment as she touched ground.

'It would have been different if I'd come to be a student. I would have had clear goals, a programme to follow . . .'

With no programme, she sat in the vault of her sister's house, staring listlessly at television.

'I was terrified. I felt locked in that house for an entire year. I hated to go out. I was cut off from all my friends. I could read English, not well, but I could read it—but I couldn't speak it . . . hardly a word. I felt I was blind and deaf. My self-esteem was totally gone. Totally. I was in America, but I wasn't part of this society at all.

'I was a huge mess of inertia. I was *stopped*—you know? like a clock? I slept and slept. Sometimes I slept eighteen hours a day. I'd go to bed at night, and it would be dark again when I woke up.'

During that year, Insook's whole family—parents, brothers,

cousins—came to America by separate planes. They were scattered across the land mass, between Washington State and Detroit.

'There was no going back. I had no home to return to. I had come here to *live* and I felt suicidal. That sense of homelessness . . . you know? You have no past—that's been taken away from you. You have no present—you are doing nothing. *Nothing*. And you have no future. The pain of it—do you understand?'

Yet even at the bottom of this pit of unbeing, Insook saw one spark of tantalizing possibility. On television, and on her rare, alarmed ventures on to the streets, she watched American women with wonder.

'Oh, but they were such marvellous creatures! I would see them working . . . driving cars . . . talking. They were so confident! Free! Carefree! Not afraid! And I was . . . *me*.'

The prospect of these women made English itself infinitely desirable. Korean was the language of patriarchy and submission; English the language of liberation and independence. Insook had school-English. It worked on paper; she could write a letter in it, even, with some difficulty, read a book. But its spoken form bore hardly any relationship at all to the English spoken on American streets. She followed the news programmes on TV (she was through with fictions), and parroted back the words as the announcers said them. She practised, haltingly, in the stores.

I said that I marvelled at her articulacy now. 'You're saying things with such precision, and complex, emotional things too. You're making me feel inarticulate, and I've spent forty-seven years living inside this language.'

'Oh, it is so much more easy for a Korean woman to learn than for a Korean man. She can afford to make mistakes. When a man makes a mistake, it is an affront to his masculine pride, to his great Koreanness. He is programmed to feel shame. So he learns six sentences, six grammatical forms, and sticks to them. He's safe inside this little language; his pride is not wounded. But when a woman makes mistakes, everybody laughs. She's "just a girl"— she's being "cute". So she can dare things that a man wouldn't begin to try, for fear of making a fool of himself. I could make a fool of myself . . . so it was easy for me to learn English.'

It was still three years before she felt 'comfortable' about leaving the house, and four before she began to make her first

American friends. She had gone to stay at the family house of a cousin in Bellingham, at the north end of Puget Sound, where she went to college to study for a diploma in nursing.

At Bellingham, Insook began to go on dates with American men.

'My brothers came to see me. They felt betrayed. Korean males—you must know this—are the most conservative on this earth. For me to be seen alone in a café, talking to a white American man, that was a deep, deep insult to them. I was insulting their maleness, insulting their pride, insulting everything that "Korea" meant to them. They threatened me . . .'

A year later, Insook announced her engagement, to an American.

'My father said, "I will disown you"' she smiled—a sad, complicated shrug of a smile. 'So I said . . .' For the first time since we'd been talking, she produced a pack of cigarettes and lit one. 'I said, "I am sick and tired of this family. OK, disown me. *Please* disown me!"'

The brothers came round, with a fraternal warning.

They promised me that they would bomb the church where we were getting married. We had to hire security guards. One of my brothers said he would prefer to blow me up, blow me to pieces, than see me married to an American.'

'And you really believed that he meant it—that he'd make a bomb?'

'Oh, yes. My brothers weren't doing well. They were struggling in America. They were just fighting me with what little ego they had left . . .'

The wedding went ahead, with security guards. At the last moment one of the brothers turned up, shamefaced, with a gift.

Her marriage was 'absolutely democratic', and it was, thought Insook, the prospect of this democracy that her father and brothers had so feared and hated. 'For the Korean man, everything that he is, his whole being, is in direct conflict with what this society is about.'

A little Korean culture had survived in Insook's American marriage. She and her husband left their shoes by the front door and went around the house barefoot or in stockings. They lived closer to the ground than most Americans. 'He has a naturally floor-oriented lifestyle.' She sometimes cooked Korean food. 'He likes to use chopsticks.' Her husband had 'a few phrases' of Korean.

'But I seldom feel my identity as a Korean now. I forget that I look different—'

'You think you look "different"? Look at all of us here—' We were sitting in a booth at the Queen City Grill on First, a favourite lunch-spot for Seattle's wine-drinking, seafood-eating, stylish middle class. We had melting-pot faces: at almost every table, you could see a mop of Swedish hair, an Anglo-Saxon mouth, an Italian tan, Chinese-grandmother eyes, a high Slav cheek-bone. In this company, Insook's appearance was in the classic American grain.

'No, you're right. It's when people know I come from Korea, I sometimes get deadlocked in arguments. The moment someone knows I am a Korean, then I'm framed in their stereotype of how a Korean ought to be. Like, if I'm shy for some reason, then it's "Of course you're shy—that's so *Korean*." But then again, if I am outspoken, if I get angry in a discussion, that's "being Korean" too. Whatever I do, it must be "Korean". I do get mad over that sometimes.'

Yet Insook's attachment to Korea still went deep. It would sometimes take her by surprise. Shopping in the Bon, she felt 'shame' (that most powerful of all Korean words) when she saw how Korean products were almost always shoddier than their Japanese or American counterparts.

'They are made to fall apart in a few months, and I think, *this is my country*—'

'But your country is America now.'

'No, I still identify with Korea. I do still think of myself as a foreigner and of America as a foreign country. Not on the surface. In a profound way, that I can't change. I think, too, that my sense of root is beginning to return. Just lately, I've been taking up calligraphy again . . . And I'd like to do something for the Korean community here. When I see other Koreans in Seattle, I know that we've all been through the same pain, the same suffering, and I feel good that I went through that pain . . . it's very important for me.'

She was doing what she could. For Korean patients in the hospital where she worked, she was translator, legal advisor, counsellor, kind heart. That morning, she had been trying to find a lawyer who would take on the case of a Korean who had been injured at work and whose employer had refused to pay him compensation.

'But I do feel uncomfortable with other Korean people. There's so much suspicion and resentment. To so many of them, I am not *me*, I am a girl who married an American. As soon as I tell them my American name, I see it in their eyes. I am *one of those*.'

'But you still go on trying—'

'I feel compulsion—compulsion? compassion? I don't know, I suppose both for Korea. You know? It's like having two friends . . . There is the rich friend, who's doing very well in life. You're always glad to see him; you're happy in his company . . . But you don't need to worry about him. That's like America is for me. Then I have this poor friend. Always in some kind of trouble. It depresses me to have to meet him. But . . . he is the friend who needs me. That is Korea.'

Some days later, I was talking to Jay Park again. A year after he'd arrived in Seattle, he'd met a Korean girl (at the Presbyterian church), and they'd married in '67, driving off in the pale blue T-Bird with electric windows. They now had two sons and a daughter.

It was odd, Jay Park said, that while nearly all of his sons' friends were Korean, 'eighty per cent' of his daughter's friends were American. 'She just seem to like to hang out with white Americans . . .'

I could hear Insook's voice, talking of 'marvellous creatures'.

'How do you take to the idea of a white American son-in-law?' I asked.

Jay Park laughed. 'I deal with that one awready. I tell her. "Day you bring home American boyfriend, that's the day you dead meat, girl!"'

It was a joke. He was hamming the role of heavy Korean father, but there was enough seriousness in it to give it an uncomfortable edge.

'Dead meat!' His laugh faded into a deep frown. 'I see these intermarriage families, and always is some . . . *unsatisfied* . . . *life*. You get what I am saying now? I am thinking our kids got lost somewhere . . . somewhere between the cultures.'

All back issues are now in print and available at £5.99 each (including postage) from Granta, Dept BIS32, 2/3 Hanover Yard, Noel Road, Islington, London N1 8BE, or from all branches of Waterstones. Credit card orders can be accepted by phone on (071) 704 0470.

Notes on Contributors

Simon Schama is Professor of History at Harvard University. He is the author of *Citizens: A Chronicle of the French Revolution* and *The Embarrassment of Riches*. His forthcoming books include one on landscape in history and a study of Rembrandt. **Julian Barnes's** previous contribution to *Granta*, 'Emma Bovary's Eyes', appeared in issue 7, 'The Best of Young British Novelists'. His most recent book is *The History of the World in 10½ Chapters*. **Richard Holmes's** biography of Coleridge won the Whitbread Prize for book of the year. His piece in this issue is drawn from the book he is currently writing, *Johnson and Savage: A Biographical Mystery*, which will be published next spring by Hodder & Stoughton. His piece 'In Stevenson's Footsteps', based on the travels of Robert Louis Stevenson, appeared in *Granta* 10, 'Travel Writing'. 'Sovinec in Moravia' are the first photographs published by **Jindrich Streit** in this country. Streit, forty-three, continues to live and work in the village of Sovinec. **Elizabeth Hardwick** was born in Kentucky and lives in New York City. Her books include *Seduction and Betrayal* and *Sleepless Nights*. **Jonathan Spence** teaches Chinese history at Yale University, where he is currently a MacArthur Fellow. His book *The Search for Modern China* was published in May. The twin brothers **Giorgio and Nicola Pressburger** were born in Budapest in 1937. 'The Temple in Budapest' is included in a collection of stories entitled *Homage to the Eighth District* that will be published by Readers International in the summer. Nicola Pressburger died in 1985. Giorgio Pressburger's next collection, *The Law of the White Spaces*, will be published by Granta Books in 1991. **Allan Gurganus** is the author of *Oldest Living Confederate Widow Tells All*. **Gore Vidal** lives in Italy. He has been working on *Epistle to the New Age*, from which this story is taken, since 1987. Five decades of **Martha Gellhorn's** peace-time journalism *The View from the Ground* is published by Granta Books (£13.99). Martha Gellhorn lives in North Wales. As this issue goes to press, **Jonathan Raban** is somewhere in the Florida Keys. The four parts of 'New World' are from a book entitled *Hunting Mister Heartbreak* that will be published by Collins Harvill in November and Harper & Row in the United States next spring.